ZONDERVAN

DICTIONARY

of BIBLE and

THEOLOGY WORDS

ZONDERVAN

DICTIONARY

of BIBLE and
THEOLOGY WORDS

MATTHEW S. DEMOSS
AND J. EDWARD MILLER

ZONDERVAN

ZONDERVAN.com/
AUTHORTRACKER
follow your favorite authors

ZONDERVAN®

Zondervan Dictionary of Bible and Theology Words
Copyright © 2002 by Matthew S. DeMoss and J. Edward Miller

Requests for information should be addressed to:

Zondervan, *Grand Rapids, Michigan 49530*

Library of Congress Cataloging-in-Publication Data

DeMoss, Matthew S., 1969-
  Zondervan dictionary of Bible and theology words / Matthew S. DeMoss
and J. Edward Miller.
    p. cm.
    ISBN-10: 0-310-24034-4 (pbk.)
    ISBN-13: 978-0-310-24034-1 (pbk.)
    1. Theology—Dictionaries. 2. Bible—Dictionaries. I. Miller, J. Edward, 1972-   II. Title.
BR95 .D44 2002
220.3—dc21   2001006892
                                        CIP

Interior design by Nancy Wilson

Printed in the United States of America

This book is dedicated
affectionately to our wives,
Jenny Miller and Lori DeMoss

CONTENTS

INTRODUCTION

Studying the Bible is like traveling overseas—though fascinating and life-changing, it's not always a smooth transition. There are language barriers, curious cultural differences, unfamiliar terrain (not to mention people), and a sense of uncertainty about almost everything one encounters. You will see them—courageous tourists determined to overcome these obstacles, scrutinizing maps on street corners and poring over guidebooks for tips. People who read the Bible need similar help.

This book is like a map or a guidebook for those who want to maximize their study of God's Word. As the title suggests, it contains two broad categories of entries: biblical terms and theological terms—that is, difficult words that one encounters in the Bible itself as well as the terminology derived from Bible study in theology.

Unlike other tools that emphasize the people and places of the Bible, this book deals with terms that pertain to Old Testament introduction (e.g., "P," "deutero-Isaiah"), New Testament introduction (e.g., "Apocrypha," "Pauline," "Q"), Hebrew grammar (e.g., "construct relationship," "vowel pointing"), Greek grammar (e.g., "anarthrous," "perfect"), Old Testament exegesis and interpretation (e.g., "covenant," "Messiah"), New Testament exegesis and interpretation (e.g., "pericope," "redaction criticism"), and theological terms of all sorts (e.g., "propitiation," "ecclesiology," "original sin," "pretribulationism," "speaking in tongues"). The definitions—even for highly specialized terms—are concise and easy-to-understand for people who have never been to seminary.

This dictionary helps users to navigate not only the Bible but also other Bible study tools aimed at the nonprofessional reader (e.g., commentaries and Bible dictionaries). Often dust jackets describe a book's audience as including everyone from pastors to laypeople, from those who are well-versed in biblical studies to those who are just getting started. But what happens when those with no formal training try to use one of these books? Inevitably they stumble upon a large amount of specialized vocabulary that impedes their understanding. This book is a companion volume, coming alongside other tools to give readers help when needed—that is, whenever strange words crop up.

This book is extensively cross-referenced to help readers find entries related to the words they look up. Any term in SMALL CAPS is a separate entry itself. Only the first occurrence of a word in a definition is marked as such. Also, because of the variations in terminology, a large number of "pointers" have been included to make sure readers find the help they need. In addition, innumerable biblical references have been included. These provide a solid basis for the definitions and refer the reader to the pertinent biblical passages for further study.

The authors wish you well as you embark on this journey through the exotic and surprising terrain of the Bible. We hope you make some marvelous discoveries.

Matthew S. DeMoss and J. Edward Miller

A.D. Abbreviation of the Latin *anno Domini*, "in the year of the Lord." When used, this abbreviation precedes the year (e.g., A.D. 70). The designation C.E., "common era," conveys the same time description in nonreligious language.

a fortiori A logical argument in which a conclusion is shown to be even more certain than a previous one; a "how much more" statement (Lat., "from the stronger"). For example, "If you then, though you are evil, know how to give good gifts to your children, *how much more* will your Father in heaven give the Holy Spirit to those who ask him" (Luke 11:13). See also QAL WAHOMER.

a posteriori In logic, denoting reasoning that is based on observation or experience instead of theory (Lat., "from the latter"). See also A PRIORI.

a priori In logic, denoting reasoning that is based on theory instead of observation or experience (Lat., "from the former"). See also A POSTERIORI.

Aaronic priesthood The line of Israelite priests traced through Aaron's two younger sons, Eleazar and Ithamar (Ex. 28:1; Lev. 3:2–4). In Hebrews 7 the Aaronic priesthood is contrasted with the priestly role of Jesus, who comes from "the order of Melchizedek." Leviticus 8–10 records the inauguration of Aaron's priestly dynasty, also referred to as the "sons of Aaron."

Abaddon   In the Old Testament, the place of destruction (Heb., *abaddon*, "destruction"), the place of the dead, or the grave (see Job 28:22; Ps. 88:11; Prov. 27:20). In its one New Testament appearance, the word serves as a title for the angel of the ABYSS (Rev. 9:11). See also HADES and SHEOL.

abba   Aramaic for "father." Jesus may have been the first to address God with this word, for in Jewish literature prior to the New Testament period the term was used of fathers and rabbis, but never of God. In its three New Testament occurrences (Mark 14:36; Rom. 8:15; Gal. 4:6) the term is immediately followed by the word "father."

A

abide   To stay, rest, or remain. In Christian vernacular the word usually refers to one's responsibility to Christ based on John 15:1–11 (see also 1 John 2:24–28; 4:13). Some, however, understand the passages that speak of "abiding" as referring to SALVATION rather than to the believer's commitment.

ablative   In Greek, a use of the GENITIVE case that denotes separation, usually requiring the preposition "from" when translated into English. While some consider the ablative a separate case from the genitive (i.e., EIGHT-CASE SYSTEM), most subsume the ablative under the broad heading of "genitive" (i.e., FIVE-CASE SYSTEM).

ablution   Ceremonial washing of one's body, clothing, or other objects for spiritual purification (see Ex. 19:10; Lev. 17:15–16; Mark 7:4; Heb. 9:10). See also CEREMONIALLY UNCLEAN.

abomination of desolation   A term that appears in Daniel (11:31; 12:11; see also 9:27) and describes an abominable, devastating act. Some translations unpack the expression as "the abomination that causes desolation." Likely it is a reference to Antiochus IV's defilement of the temple in 167 B.C.E., which led to the MACCABEAN REVOLT (1 Macc. 1:54). The New Testament quotations of

OF BIBLE AND THEOLOGY WORDS

this expression (Matt. 24:15; Mark 13:14) are commonly understood as referring to the destruction of the temple in 70 C.E. or to
a yet future act that has been foreshadowed in these incidents
(2 Thess. 2:3–4).

Abrahamic covenant The unconditional promise of God
to give Abraham physical descendants and the land stretching
from the River of Egypt (the Nile River, or perhaps Wadi el-Arish
in the Sinai Peninsula) to the Euphrates River. The COVENANT is
first mentioned in Genesis 12:1–3; it is reaffirmed and described
in greater detail in subsequent passages (13:14–17; 15:4–7, 18–
21; 17:1–27; 22:17–18), including the rite of CIRCUMCISION
(17:9–14).

Abram Original name of Abraham, meaning "exalted father"
(Gen. 17:5).

absolute state In Hebrew, the condition of a NOUN that is
so closely linked to the preceding word or words that they are
counted together, and whose TRANSLATION usually requires the
English PREPOSITION "of" (e.g., "sorrows" in "man of sorrows," Isa.
53:3). See also CONSTRUCT STATE.

abyss A bottomless pit, the underworld, or simply the place of
the dead, especially when occupied by demons (see Luke 8:31;
Rev. 9:11; 11:7; 17:8; 20:1, 3; see also Rom. 10:7, where it is translated "the deep").

accusative In Greek, the CASE that normally marks a word as
the DIRECT OBJECT of the VERB.

acrostic A literary device in which lines, verses, or sections
begin with consecutive letters of the alphabet. Acrostic poetry
occurs a number of times in the OLD TESTAMENT (e.g., Pss. 111;
112; 119; Prov. 31:10–31; Lam. 1–4), but it is lost in translation.

A

13

active voice In Greek, the VOICE that conveys that the subject is the doer or the cause of the verbal action, as opposed to the PASSIVE VOICE, in which the subject is the receiver of the verbal action. Using various verbal patterns, Hebrew can convey the same thing.

adiaphora Ethical or practical matters that are neither commanded nor forbidden in the Bible and are therefore morally neutral (Gk., "things indifferent"). Many classify styles of church music as *adiaphora*.

adjective A word that modifies a NOUN or a state of being. For example, "good" modifies "shepherd" in "I am the good shepherd" (John 10:11).

Adonai A particular form of a common Hebrew word meaning "lord" that is used as one of the OLD TESTAMENT names for God, translated "Lord" (e.g., Ps. 109:21). Although the common word *ʾadon* often refers to human masters (e.g., Num. 32:25), nearly every use of the specific form *ʾadonay* refers to God. Out of reverence for the name of God, those reading the biblical text often substituted the title "Adonai" for the divine name "YAHWEH."

adoption To take another's child and legally make him/her one's own. In the New Testament, adoption is described as one of the benefits of salvation (John 1:12; Gal. 4:4–5; Eph. 1:5). It speaks of the new standing that Christians enjoy, including access to God the Father (Rom. 8:15), a share in the divine inheritance (Rom. 8:17, 23), and the responsibility that comes from being God's children (Eph. 5:1; Phil. 2:15; Heb. 12:5–9). The word appears only in Paul's letters.

adoptionism The view that the man Jesus at his baptism was adopted by God and thus became divine. Adoptionist Christology was promoted in Spain in the eighth century but condemned

14

at church councils. It has precedents in EBIONITISM, GNOSTICISM, and DYNAMIC MONARCHIANISM.

Advent   An arrival or coming, especially the coming of Jesus Christ. First Advent refers to the INCARNATION; Second Advent refers to the SECOND COMING. In some traditions the expression designates the period of time from four Sundays before Christmas until Christmas.

A

adverb   A word that modifies a VERB, an ADJECTIVE, or another adverb, indicating such things as manner, time, duration, intensity, and so on. For example, when Jesus invited Simon and Andrew to follow him, Mark 1:18 emphasizes their abrupt response with an adverb: "*At once* they left their nets and followed him."

adverbial   Of, related to, or functioning like an ADVERB.

adversary   An enemy or opponent (Matt. 5:25). In 1 Peter 5:8 the term is used of the DEVIL. See also SATAN.

advocate   A helper, defender, comforter, or counselor. The title is normally associated with Jesus (1 John 2:1) or the Holy Spirit (John 14:16, 26; 15:26; 16:7). See PARACLETE.

agape   The most common New Testament word for love, used of God's love for people (Rom. 5:8; Eph. 3:19; 1 John 3:1) as well as of believers' love for God and for one another (John 13:35; 15:13; 1 Cor. 13:1–3; 1 John 4:11). Also a common meal shared among early Christians (Jude 12).

age of accountability   According to some theologians, the age when children become accountable to God for their moral choices (see Deut. 1:39; 2 Sam. 12:22–23; Mark 10:13–16). Also called the AGE OF REASON.

age of reason A designation for the eighteenth century in the Western world, when rationalism—the philosophy that truth can be known through the power of human reason—became widespread; i.e., the Enlightenment. The term is also equivalent to the AGE OF ACCOUNTABILITY.

age-day theory See DAY-AGE THEORY.

agnosticism The system or worldview that says it is not possible to know with certainty about God's existence, things unseen, or the afterlife (Gk., *agnosis*, "no knowledge").

agrapha Plural of AGRAPHON.

agraphon A saying of Jesus that is not found in Matthew, Mark, Luke, or John (Gk., *agrapha*, "unwritten"). "It is more blessed to give than to receive" is a well-known example (Acts 20:35).

Akedah Hebrew word meaning "binding," usually associated with the binding of Isaac by Abraham in preparation for his sacrifice (see Gen. 22:9). Through this story, this word became associated with God's provision of a substitute—the principle of one person or animal being sacrificed for another. Also spelled Aqedah.

Akkadian An ancient SEMITIC language that was spoken in BABYLONIA and ASSYRIA. Akkadian literature provides background information for Old Testament studies and insight on its sister languages, HEBREW and ARAMAIC, the languages of the Old Testament.

Aktionsart In Greek, the nature of the action of a VERB (i.e., duration, repetition, or completion), as opposed to the time of the action (past, present, or future). New Testament scholars usually distinguish *Aktionsart* from verbal ASPECT, in that *Aktionsart* represents the nature of a verb's action in a specific syntactical context while aspect pertains to verbal action inherent in a given tense (Germ., *Aktionsart,* "aspect").

aleph   The first letter of the HEBREW alphabet.

Alexandrian text-type   A term from TEXTUAL CRITICISM that designates a highly regarded form of the New Testament text traceable to Alexandria, Egypt. As the New Testament was copied and recopied, three distinct forms of the text, named for their supposed place of origin, developed: Byzantine, Western, and Alexandrian. The Alexandrian text-type is generally regarded as the closest to the ORIGINAL. See also BYZANTINE TEXT-TYPE and WESTERN TEXT-TYPE.

Alexandrian school   A center of Christian scholarship in Alexandria, Egypt, that flourished from the second to the fourth century, emphasizing ALLEGORICAL INTERPRETATION of the Bible. Clement, Origen, and Athanasius all taught at Alexandria. See also ANTIOCHENE SCHOOL.

Alexandrinus   See CODEX ALEXANDRINUS.

alien   In the Old Testament, someone who was not a member of a particular community (usually ISRAEL) and thus did not enjoy the privileges of membership (see Gen. 19:9; Lev. 16:29). A number of passages address the rights of aliens and how they were to be treated fairly (Ex. 22:21; 23:9; Lev. 19:33–34; Deut. 10:18–19; 24:14, 17–18; Jer. 7:6; 22:3; Ezek. 22:7, 29; Mal. 3:5). In the New Testament believers are called aliens (1 Peter 1:1; 2:11) and referred to as heavenly, not earthly, citizens (see Phil. 3:20; Heb. 11:8–16).

allegorical interpretation   An approach to biblical interpretation in which the literal meaning is secondary to some symbolic meaning. Allegorical interpretation is associated with ORIGEN (c. 185–c. 254) and the ALEXANDRIAN SCHOOL.

A

allegory   A literary device in which an event, object, or character is employed to represent symbolically a person or idea (see Gal. 4:24).

alleluia   See HALLELUJAH.

alms   Money given to the poor as an expression of religious devotion (Matt. 6:1–4; Acts 3:2–3; 10:2–4, 31; 24:17). In the Old Testament alms came in the form of goods and produce generously given to or designated for the less fortunate (Lev. 19:9–10; Deut. 14:28–29).

alpha   The first letter of the GREEK alphabet.

Alpha and Omega   Title for God signifying his eternality, represented by the first and last letters of the GREEK alphabet; the first and the last (Rev. 1:8; 21:6; 22:13).

already-not yet   An approach to biblical interpretation of eschatological passages that states that while certain prophecies are initiated or partially fulfilled, their ultimate fulfillments are yet future.

altar   A structure upon which sacrifices are offered or incense is burned in the worship of some deity. The earliest Old Testament altars were apparently erected for commemoration and/or sacrifice (see Gen. 8:20; 33:20; Ex. 17:15). The TABERNACLE specifications called for one altar for burnt offerings (Ex. 38:1–7) and another for incense (Ex. 30:1–10), and these instructions were largely followed while furnishing the temple.

amanuensis   A person who takes dictation or writes on behalf of another. For example, Tertius served as Paul's amanuensis for the writing of Romans (Rom. 16:22).

ambassador   An authoritative political representative who speaks or acts on behalf of a nation or its ruler; an envoy. In the Bible, ambassadors were dispatched to carry messages, including protests (Judg. 11:12–23), to request favors (Num. 20:14–17; Judg. 11:17, 19), to form alliances and make treaties (Josh. 9:4–6), to solicit help (1 Kings 5:3–6), and to offer congratulations (2 Sam. 8:10; 1 Kings 5:1), among other things. In the New Testament, Paul says that believers are "Christ's ambassadors" (2 Cor. 5:20).

A

amen   A Hebrew derivative denoting firmness or certainty, which came to be used in a variety of contexts, including confirmation of an oath (Deut. 27:15–26; Jer. 11:5) and as a response in worship or after prayer (Pss. 41:13; 106:48; Rom. 11:36; 1 Tim. 6:16). Jesus frequently used it to introduce a saying (Matt. 16:28; Luke 4:24; John 5:25; sometimes translated "truly" or "verily"). Jesus himself is called "the Amen" in Revelation 3:14.

amillennialism   The view that the mention of one thousand years in Revelation 20 does not refer to an actual period of time but rather to the reign of Christ figuratively. In this view the GREAT WHITE THRONE JUDGMENT (Rev. 20:11–15) immediately follows the SECOND COMING (Rev. 19:11–16). See also MILLEN- NIUM, POSTMILLENNIALISM, and PREMILLENNIALISM.

Amoraim   Jewish scribes who produced the TALMUD during the third, fourth, and fifth centuries C.E.

amulet   An object worn as jewelry for superstitious reasons.

anabaptism   BAPTISM a second time, usually underwent by adults who received baptism as infants (Gk., "rebaptism").

anachronism   A word, person, or event wrongly placed in time (Gk., "back[ward] time").

anacoluthon The interruption of a sentence by another grammatical construction (Gk., "inconsistent"). For example, in Ephesians 3:1–2 Paul interrupts his sentence with an abrupt grammatical shift.

anagogy An allusion or statement pertaining to HEAVEN or the afterlife. While the Old Testament has few (Pss. 16:10; 49:15; Isa. 26:19; Dan. 12:2), the New Testament is replete with them (Matt. 5:12; 6:20; Luke 15:18; 1 Cor. 15:20–24; Eph. 3:15; Phil. 3:20–21; 2 Tim. 4:18; Rev. 21:1). In medieval EXEGESIS, the anagogical sense of Scripture pertained to its mystical, moral, or spiritual meaning or application. Also anagoge.

Anakim The race of giants that the twelve Israelite emissaries encountered while spying out Canaan (Num. 13:28, 33; Deut. 1:28). The Anakim were later conquered by Joshua (Josh. 11:21–22) and Caleb (Josh. 14:12, 15; 15:13–14; Judg. 1:20) and expelled from Hebron and the surrounding hill country. Goliath probably descended from this people, who trace their lineage to Anak and, ultimately, the NEPHILIM (Num. 13:33; cf. Gen. 6:4). Also called the Anakites.

anarthrous Not having an article. The opposite of ARTHROUS.

anathema A Greek word denoting strong denunciation or a CURSE, or signifying the object of a curse (see Rom. 9:3; 1 Cor. 12:3; Gal. 1:8–9). Paul uses this word in 1 Corinthians 16:22 as a curse on those who do not love Jesus Christ.

ancient Near East Designation for both a time period, extending from the earliest periods until approximately the fall of Babylon in 539 B.C.E., as well as a large geographical region roughly equivalent to the contemporary term "Middle East." It includes such countries as modern-day Iran, Iraq, Israel, Jordan, Lebanon, Syria, Turkey, Egypt, and countries on the Arabian Peninsula.

20

Ancient of Days   Title for YAHWEH that portrays God as elderly (lit., "aged in days"; see Dan. 7:9, 13, 22).

angel   A supernatural messenger or agent of God (Gk., "messenger"). While most are holy, some angels are wicked, having sinned and received their punishment from God (2 Peter 2:4). In the Old Testament, angels sometimes protected ISRAEL (2 Kings 19:35). They also announced special births, such as Samson's (Judg. 13:3–5), John the Baptist's (Luke 1:11–17), and Jesus' (Luke 1:28–33). Scripture forbids the worship of angels (Col. 2:18). See also ANGEL OF THE LORD.

angel of death   Designation for the "destroyer" sent by the Lord during the PASSOVER to kill the firstborn in homes where the doorposts were not marked with Lamb's blood (Ex. 12:23). Some also think that Job 33:22 refers to the angel of death.

angel of the Lord   In the Old Testament, a heavenly messenger sent as God's personal spokesman. Some have identified him as a mere ANGEL who speaks in behalf of God, while others think this a technical term for the preincarnate CHRIST or for God himself, because of the angel's identification with God in many passages and his speech, often as God in the first person (Gen. 16:7–14; 22:11–18; Ex. 3:2–5; Judg. 6:11–23; Zech. 3:1–7).

angelology   The branch of THEOLOGY concerned with the study of angels, both fallen and unfallen.

animism   Any of various worldviews that sees natural objects and phenomena as animated by spirits, disembodied souls, or gods. This strong association of the physical and the spiritual worlds results in animists attempting to manipulate the spirit world by manipulating the physical world, and vice versa.

annihilationism In ESCHATOLOGY, the view that the wicked will not suffer in HELL forever but will be destroyed, either upon death or after a short period of suffering in the afterlife. Also called conditioned immortality.

anno Domini Latin term meaning "in the year of the Lord," abbreviated A.D. See also A.D.

Annunciation, the Traditional name for Gabriel's announcement to Mary that she would give birth to Jesus (Luke 1:26–38).

anoint To apply oil as part of a religious rite that consecrates someone or something to God. In the Old Testament kings, priests, and prophets were often anointed when they were inaugurated, as were the TABERNACLE and its utensils (Ex. 30:25–33). In addition, perfumed oil was used in bathing and to anoint the dead for burial.

Anselmic Pertaining to the scholastic theologian Anselm (1033–1109 C.E.) or his teachings. Anselm, BISHOP of Canterbury, is remembered for his articulation of the ONTOLOGICAL ARGUMENT for the existence of God and for his SATISFACTION THEORY OF THE ATONEMENT, which emphasized God's satisfaction with Christ's substitutionary death.

antagonist A literary term for the individual in a story who opposes the central character. For example, in the book of Esther Haman, the antagonist, opposed Esther, Mordecai, and ultimately the entire Jewish nation.

antediluvian Denoting the period of time before the GENESIS FLOOD (Lat., *ante*, "before," and *diluvium*, "flood").

antetype See ANTITYPE.

22

OF BIBLE AND THEOLOGY WORDS

anthropological argument   An argument used to prove the existence of a moral and intelligent God based on the moral and intelligent nature of humankind (Gk., *anthropos*, "human being").

anthropology   In THEOLOGY, the study of humankind, including aspects such as sin, sociological matters, and the material and immaterial nature of persons (Gk., *anthropos*, "human being").

A

anthropomorphism   The attributing of human characteristics, actions, or behavior to God (Gk., *anthropos*, "human being," and *morphe*, "shape" or "form").

anthropopathism   The attributing of human emotions and feelings to God (Gk., *anthropos*, "human being," and *pathos*, "emotion" or "feeling").

antichrist   The title given generally to anyone who opposes Christ, his authority, or his coming in the flesh (1 John 2:18; 2 John 7). Also the title used to designate the primary eschatological enemy of Christ (taking *anti* to mean "against"), or the one seeking to take upon himself the glory and honor that is due Christ (taking *anti* to mean "in place of"). Found only in the letters of John.

antilegomena   Early church designation for books whose acceptance into the CANON was disputed (Gk., "spoken against"), such as 2 Peter and the *Epistle of Barnabas*.

antinomianism   The view that Christians, because of the abundance of God's grace, are free from obligation to any MORAL LAW (Gk., *anti*, "against," *nomos*, "law"). Though attributed to Paul by his opponents (Rom. 3:8), Paul himself writes elsewhere against such a licentious lifestyle (Rom. 6:1–2, 14–16; Gal. 5:13).

antinomy   In philosophy and THEOLOGY, a pair of seemingly contradictory concepts of equal validity (Gk., *anti*, "against," *nomos*, "law"). For example, God's sovereignty and human freedom seem incompatible, yet both appear to be true and biblically defensible.

Antiochene school   A center of Christian scholarship in Antioch that flourished from the third to the fifth century, emphasizing, in response to the ALEXANDRIAN SCHOOL, literal interpretation of the Bible. Theophilus of Antioch, Diodore of Tarsus, and John Chrysostom are representative of Antiochene HERMENEUTICS.

anti-Semitism   Hostility toward or persecution of Jews. While such hostility has long existed (see Est. 3:6; 9:24), Christian anti-Semitism over the last two millennia has sometimes been fueled by the belief that the Jews were responsible for killing Jesus (see John 18:28–19:16).

antithetic parallelism   Literary device employed frequently in the poetic portions of the Old Testament (usually the Psalms), in which something is stated positively in the first of a pair of lines and negatively in the second (e.g., Pss. 1:6; 90:6). See PARALLELISM.

antitype   The object or person prefigured by a TYPE. Often the antitype is Christ, foreshadowed by an Old Testament event or figure (e.g., Adam, 1 Cor. 15:45–49; Melchizedek, Heb. 7). See also TYPOLOGICAL INTERPRETATION.

aorist tense   In Greek, the TENSE that portrays an action in summary, without disclosing the duration of that action. As such, the aorist points to the reality of an action, not its nature.

apocalypse   A literary GENRE in which the hidden purposes of God are revealed and the last judgment is emphasized. In general, apocalypses (1) are set within a narrative framework and (2) involve revelation about transcendental realities through (3) visions or other-worldly journeys. Also referred to as apocalyptic. Also used as the title of the New Testament book of Revelation (Gk., *apokalypsis*, "revelation").

apocatastasis Restoration, particularly future; universal restoration as described in the Bible (Eph. 1:9–10; Phil. 2:10–11). Some have understood this to include universal SALVATION. Also written as apokatastasis. See UNIVERSALISM.

Apocrypha Group of ancient Jewish books resembling the books of the canonical Old Testament though not a part of it (Gk., *apokrypha*, "hidden things"). These writings, excluded from the Protestant CANON but included in those of Roman Catholicism and Eastern Orthodoxy, include Tobit, Judith, the Wisdom of Solomon, Sirach, Baruch, and 1–2 Maccabees, among others. Also known as Old Testament apocrypha or deuterocanonical books. The related term "apocryphal" is sometimes used of the OT PSEUDEPIGRAPHA, THE NT PSEUDEPIGRAPHA, and the APOSTOLIC FATHERS.

apodosis The "then" CLAUSE of a CONDITIONAL SENTENCE (i.e., one that contains an if–then construction). The second clause in this verse is the apodosis: "If there is no resurrection of the dead, then not even Christ has been raised" (1 Cor. 15:13). It is the counterpart of the PROTASIS.

Apollinarianism A fourth-century view promoted by Laodicean BISHOP Apollinarius (c. 310–390), who taught that in place of a human mind (*nous*) CHRIST had the divine LOGOS. Thus the incarnate Christ was only two-thirds human, having a human body and SOUL, but a divine mind. Apollinarianism was officially condemned at the Second Ecumenical Council at Constantinople in 381 C.E.

ZONDERVAN DICTIONARY

Apollyon The Greek equivalent of the Hebrew word "ABAD-DON" (see Rev. 9:11).

apologetics The defense of the Christian faith against attacks, criticisms, and objections (Gk., *apologia*, "defense"). Apologists employ logic and reason while considering the evidence supporting Christianity.

apophatic theology An approach to THEOLOGY that stresses the inability of language to explain God in human categories. It asserts the inadequacy of human understanding and the "otherness" of the Divine. Sometimes called NEGATIVE THEOLOGY. See also CATAPHATIC THEOLOGY.

apostasy Falling or turning away from one's faith. The term originally designated political defection or rebellion, but later came to be used of those departing from obedience to Christ (see 2 Thess. 2:3; 1 Tim. 4:1–3; Heb. 3:12; 6:4–6; 2 Peter 3:17).

apostle One who is sent (Gk., *apostolos*, "messenger" or "sent one"). The term may refer to the twelve disciples appointed by Christ (Matt. 10:2–4; Mark 3:14; Luke 6:13–16) or more broadly of other leaders sent out to proclaim the GOSPEL, such as Paul and Barnabas. Even Jesus, because he was sent by God, is called an apostle (Heb. 3:1).

Apostles' Creed A statement of faith with a threefold structure highlighting the TRINITY, which may have been used by the early church as a CONFESSION during baptismal ceremonies, though in a different form. The origin of the CREED in its present form cannot be determined with precision; it was not written by the apostles as legend suggests. The earliest extant text of the creed is from the early eighth century. It became prominent in the Western church and is still recited today in some traditions.

apostolic age   The church era when the apostles were alive, from the Day of PENTECOST until John's death near the end of the first century. Most scholars associate the close of this age with the close of the New Testament CANON, marking the end of SPECIAL REVELATION. Some believe that this was a heightened time of spiritual gifts (especially healing, PROPHECY, and SPEAKING IN TONGUES), which ceased at the end of this age. See also CESSATIONISM.

Apostolic Fathers   A group of second-century writings, or the individuals who produced them (who were thought to have had some contact with the apostles). These writings include the epistles of Barnabas, Clement, Hermas, Ignatius, Quadratus, Diognetus, Papias, and Polycarp, along with the *Martyrdom of Polycarp* and the *DIDACHE*.

apostolic succession   The belief that the authority exercised by the APOSTLES was handed down through a continuous line of succeeding church leaders, usually BISHOPS.

appositive   In language study, the designation for a word or phrase that renames or defines more particularly a preceding word or phrase. For example, the appositional "Christ Jesus" defines more particularly the preceding noun, "man," in 1 Timothy 2:5.

Aquila   Second-century translator of the HEBREW BIBLE known for his literal translation.

Arabah   A narrow valley encompassing the Jordan River, the Dead Sea, and the dry land between the Dead Sea and the Gulf of Aqabah (Heb., "dry"). The term as it appears in Scripture can refer to the entire valley or to one part only. Lot lived in the Arabah, which was rich in mineral deposits (Deut. 8:9) and whose future involves nourishment and fruitfulness (Ezek. 47:1–12).

Arabic   A SEMITIC language spoken in the Middle East today. Classical Arabic arose in the fourth century C.E. During biblical times, the precursors of modern Arabic are evident in such ancient languages as Epigraphic Southern Arabic. Arabic versions of the New Testament (the most well known of which is called the Peshitta) aid in TEXTUAL CRITICISM. See also VERSION.

Aramaic   A SEMITIC language closely related to HEBREW in which some of the Old Testament is written (Gen. 31:47; Ezra 4:8–6:18; 7:12–26; Jer. 10:11; Dan. 2:4b–7:28). Aramaic was likely the common language of first-century PALESTINE, including the language of Jesus (see Mark 5:41; 7:34).

Aramaism   A trait of the ARAMAIC language that comes through in the GREEK of the New Testament or SEPTUAGINT, revealing the writer's SEMITIC influence.

archangel   A high-ranking angelic being. Michael is called an archangel in Jude 9 (see also 1 Thess. 4:16).

archetype   In literary studies, an image or pattern that recurs consistently enough in literature and in life to be considered universal. In TEXTUAL CRITICISM, a MANUSCRIPT that assumedly stands behind a number of similar manuscripts.

Arianism   The fourth-century view that Christ was a created being (albeit the highest created being), thus inferior to God and not sharing the same substance as the Father. This teaching, promoted by an Alexandrian presbyter named Arius (c. 250–336), was condemned at the Council of Nicea in 325 C.E.

Aristotelianism   Philosophy originating with or based on the teachings of Aristotle (384–322 B.C.E.). Aristotelian logic, ethics, and theories of causality were revived in the twelfth and thirteenth centuries in Western Europe; Thomas Aquinas in particular worked out SYSTEMATIC THEOLOGY from an Aristotelian orientation.

OF BIBLE AND THEOLOGY WORDS

ark   The boat built by Noah ("Noah's ark," Gen. 6–9). Also the chest that contained the tablets bearing the TEN COMMANDMENTS ("the ark of the Testimony [or covenant]," e.g., Ex. 25:10–22).

ark of the covenant   See ARK.

Armageddon   A battlefield in the valley of Jezreel and the Plain of Esdraelon at the foot of the hill of Megiddo, where an apocalyptic battle between good and evil is foretold in Revelation 16:16 (Heb., *har*, "hill," and *megiddon*, "Megiddo"). The Old Testament records many previous battles here (Judg. 4–5; 7; 2 Kings 23:29).

Arminianism   The doctrines and teachings of Jacob Arminius (1560–1609), which emphasize human choice and freedom with regard to SALVATION. This contrasts with CALVINISM, which emphasizes God's sovereign choice in salvation. See also FREE WILL.

arthrous   Having an article; ARTICULAR. The opposite of ANARTHROUS.

articular   Having an article; ARTHROUS. The opposite of ANARTHROUS.

ascension   The act of ascending, going up. Christians use this term in a technical sense to describe Christ's being lifted up into the air forty days following his RESURRECTION (Acts 1:9).

ascetic   A person who, for religious convictions, leads a simple life of self-denial. Ascetics often remove themselves from society and its conveniences. Paul seems to teach against an ascetic lifestyle in Colossians 2:20–23 and 1 Timothy 4:1–5. Some have classified John the Baptist as an ascetic.

asceticism   A lifestyle of renouncing everyday comforts in exchange for a simple life of self-discipline and often solitude. See also ASCETIC.

29

ascites See DROPSY.

aseity The doctrine that God is self-existent, not dependent on anything else for his existence (Lat., *a se*, "from himself").

Asherah A Canaanite FERTILITY GODDESS, often associated with BAAL, whose idolatrous worship is explicitly forbidden in the Old Testament (Deut. 12:3; 16:21; 1 Kings 14:15, 23). The Israelites were instructed to tear down or burn the "Asherim," presumably wooden images or poles of some kind, perhaps tree stumps with the branches chopped off (Ex. 34:13; Deut. 12:3). See also ASHERAH POLE.

A

Asherah pole A wooden IMAGE used in the worship of ASHERAH, a Canaanite goddess. The Old Testament forbids Asherah worship, and God commanded the Israelites to cut down Asherah poles (Ex. 34:13).

Ashtoreth A Canaanite goddess associated with the moon and with fertility, whose worship is forbidden in the Old Testament (1 Sam. 7:3–4; 1 Kings 11:5, 33). Ashtoreth is sometimes associated with BAAL (Judg. 2:13; 10:6; 1 Sam. 12:10). Plural, Ashtoreths or Ashtaroth. Also Astarte.

aspect The feature of the TENSE system in GREEK by which the speaker's or writer's subjective perspective on the verbal action is portrayed. Greek scholars use three broad categories: progressive/internal/imperfective, summary/external/perfective, and perfect/stative. For example, the IMPERFECT tense "was walking" in Mark 5:42 denotes progressive action, while the AORIST tense "walked" in Matthew 14:29 denotes summary action. See also AKTIONSART.

assonance A literary device that employs similar sounding words, used often in Hebrew poetry.

OF BIBLE AND THEOLOGY WORDS

Assumption of Moses A Jewish pseudepigraphical text dating from the early first century C.E. containing an alleged farewell speech of Moses to Joshua in which Moses predicts what the Israelites would experience. Only a part of the text, in a Latin translation, is extant today. Also known as the *Testament of Moses*.

assurance of salvation The confidence that one has truly been saved. While some deny that this is possible to know with certainty, others look to passages like John 10:28–29 and 1 John 5:11–13 in defense of this doctrine. See also ETERNAL SECURITY.

Assyria An enemy nation of ISRAEL reaching the height of its power in the eighth to seventh centuries B.C.E. Jonah and Nahum prophesied to Assyria, which conquered the NORTHERN KINGDOM in 722 B.C.E.

Astarte See ASHTORETH.

asyndeton A literary phenomenon in which conjunctions or connectors are omitted where one would normally expect them (Gk., "not bound together"). The appearance of asyndeton in the New Testament reflects SEMITIC influence. See also POLYSYNDETON.

atheism The system or worldview that holds that there is no God.

atonement In THEOLOGY, the removal or forgiveness of SIN through a SACRIFICE, resulting in God's appeasement (Ex. 32:30–32). Atoning sacrifices described in the Old Testament are normally blood-related (Lev. 17:11), having temporary results (e.g., annual DAY OF ATONEMENT). Inanimate objects can also receive atonement (Ex. 29:36–37). In the New Testament, Christ's atoning sacrifice for sin is complete and once-for-all (Rom. 6:10; Heb. 7:27; 10:10; 1 Peter 3:18).

31

atonement cover   The covering on the ARK of the covenant. See MERCY SEAT.

Atrahasis Epic   An Akkadian flood story in which the creator-god Enki forewarns Atrahasis, a pious man, to build a boat for his family and animals in order to escape a flood brought about because the gods were otherwise unable to control humankind. After seven days the water receded, and Atrahasis offered a sacrifice to the gods.

A

Augustine   North African Christian theologian and philosopher (354–430 C.E.) who served as a bishop in the city of Hippo and wrote against MANICHAEISM and PELAGIANISM. He is known especially for his *City of God* and *Confessions*.

Augustinianism   The theological system of Augustine of Hippo (354–430 C.E.), which emphasized human DEPRAVITY, God's free bestowal of GRACE, and the necessity of divine illumination for people to know truth and beauty. Augustine is remembered especially for his discussion of SIN, SALVATION, PREDESTINATION, human freedom, God's grace, and the CHURCH.

authorial intent   The meaning that a writer gives a text. According to some interpreters, discovering the author's intent is tantamount to understanding the true meaning of a passage.

Authorized Version   Another name for the KING JAMES VERSION, first published in 1611 and dedicated to James I. The Authorized Version endured as one of the most popular English versions until the latter part of the twentieth century. Its translators, however, were limited both in their knowledge of ancient languages and in their access to more recently discovered manuscripts. Abbreviated AV.

authorship   Concern with the identity of a document's author. Since a number of biblical books were written anonymously (e.g., the Gospels), many scholars question the traditional explanation of their authorship. Still others question the authorship of biblical books bearing the alleged author's name (e.g., 2 Peter). See also PSEUDONYMITY.

autograph   An ORIGINAL handwritten document (rather than a copy).

autographa   Plural of AUTOGRAPH. Some scholars maintain that only the autographa of the Scriptures are without error.

A

avenger of blood   The next of kin to an individual murdered by premeditation. The avenger was authorized by the MOSAIC LAW to put the murderer to death (Num. 35:19).

Azazel   A scapegoat, especially the live goat in the description of the DAY OF ATONEMENT (Lev. 16:8, 10, 26). Some think Azazel was the proper name of a demon, or of Satan himself.

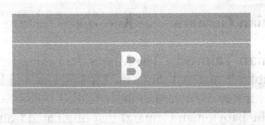

B.C.   Abbreviation of "before Christ," indicating the time before the birth of Christ. The designation B.C.E., "before common era," conveys the same time description in nonreligious language. See also A.D.

B.C.E.   See B.C.

Baal   A master or owner. The title usually refers to the Canaanite god of fertility and agriculture whose worship is forbidden in the Old Testament (Ex. 34:13–14; Deut. 7:5; Judg. 2:2). Baal was closely associated with storms, leading his subjects to offer numerous animal sacrifices so that he would bring rains and fertility to the land. The title also appears in the names of people (e.g., "Baal-Hanan," 1 Chron. 27:28) and towns (e.g., "Baal Tamar," Judg. 20:33).

Baal-zebub   See BEELZEBUB.

Babylonia   The nation in southwest Asia to which Judah was exiled (see Jer. 51:24; Ezek. 11:24). Located in present-day Iraq, Babylonia reached the height of its power beginning in 605 B.C.E. after the battle of Carchemish.

Babylonian captivity   The displacement of JUDAH from PALESTINE to BABYLONIA from 606/605 B.C.E. until roughly 536 B.C.E. Also called the Babylonian Exile or the Exile.

35

Babylonian Gemara   See BABYLONIAN TALMUD.

Babylonian Talmud   The MISHNAH, a compilation of traditional rabbinic material about the MOSAIC LAW and Jewish customs, plus interwoven commentary (called the GEMARA; or in this case the Babylonian Gemara) that originated from religious centers outside of Palestine (see PALESTINIAN TALMUD). The Talmud is of dubious value for New Testament background because commentary was still being added hundreds of years after the first centuries.

ban   Irrevocable dedication to God (Num. 18:14). Negatively, it can mean extermination ("ban" is a common English translation of the Heb. *ḥerem*, "to exterminate" or "to dedicate to God"). A ban of extermination could be invoked—usually because of idolatry—upon people (Deut. 2:34; 3:6) or places (Num. 21:2).

baptism   The ceremonial rite whereby a devotee is bathed or dipped in water (Gk., "to dip or immerse"). In the Old Testament, Jews commonly bathed or "baptized" themselves for purification (Ex. 30:17–21; Lev. 11:25). The baptism of John the Baptist was associated with REPENTANCE (Matt. 3:11). Jesus commissioned his followers to baptize others in the name of the Father, the Son, and the Holy Spirit (Matt. 28:19), probably symbolizing the believer's purification from sins.

baptism of the Holy Spirit   According to Pentecostal THEOLOGY, the initial manifestation of the Holy Spirit in the life of believers subsequent to conversion, evidenced by SPEAKING IN TONGUES (see Acts 8:15–17; 10:44–46).

baptismal formula   A standardized expression typically spoken when someone was baptized, such as, "In the name of the Father, and of the Son, and of the Holy Spirit" (Matt. 28:19).

OF BIBLE AND THEOLOGY WORDS

baptismal regeneration   The doctrine, traditionally associated with the Roman Catholic Church, that water BAPTISM is effectual for the forgiveness of sins. Some New Testament passages seem to link baptism with SALVATION (Acts 2:38; 22:16), while others intimate that faith is the only stipulation (John 3:16; Acts 5:14; Eph. 2:8).

bar-   Aramaic for "son." Peter is called Simon Bar-Jonah ("son of Jonah") in Matthew 16:17.

barbarian   Term derived from *barbaros* (Gk.) that was used by Greeks of non-Greek-speaking people (1 Cor. 14:11; here translated "foreigner") or more generally of those who were not Greek culturally (Acts 28:2–4; here translated "islanders"). In Romans 1:14 Paul uses the term as an antonym to "Greeks" (see also Col. 3:11). See also GREEK.

beatitude   A short statement communicating God's approval (Lat., "blessing"; see John 20:29). The "Beatitudes" are the collection of blessings spoken by Jesus at the beginning of the SERMON ON THE MOUNT (Matt. 5:3–11) and during the SERMON ON THE PLAIN (Luke 6:20–22). Also called MAKARISM.

Beelzebub   A title meaning "lord of flies." In the Old Testament, the term "Baal-Zebub" designates the Canaanite god BAAL (2 Kings 1:2–16). See also BEELZEBUL.

Beelzebul   A title meaning "lord of the house" or "lord of dung." In the New Testament, SATAN is called Beelzebul (Matt. 12:24–27; Mark 3:22–26; Luke 11:15–18). Many later New Testament manuscripts have replaced "Beelzebul" with "BEELZEBUB," apparently to harmonize with the Old Testament name "Baal-Zebub" (see 2 Kings 1:2–16).

behemoth   Hebrew word meaning great beast (Deut. 32:24; Pss. 49:12, 20; 50:10; Hab. 2:17). Some scholars have suggested that the behemoth in Job 40:15 is a hippopotamus. Others have proposed that the writer, drawing from mythology, had in mind a many-headed sea monster symbolizing chaos.

bema seat A throne from which a ruler pronounces judgment (Matt. 27:19; Acts 18:12; 25:10). The bema seat of Christ is where believers will receive their final judgment (Rom. 14:10; 2 Cor. 5:10). For the final judgment of unbelievers, see GREAT WHITE THRONE JUDGMENT.

B

ben- Hebrew for "son." For example, in 1 Kings 15:18, Ben-Hadad is literally "son of Hadad."

benediction A pronouncement of divine favor, usually conferred toward the end of a discourse or letter (see Heb. 13:20–21). See also BLESSING.

Benedictus Zechariah's song of thanksgiving in Luke 1:68–79 occasioned by the birth of his son, John the Baptist.

bestiality Sexual relations between humans and animals, something expressly forbidden in the Old Testament (Lev. 18:23; Deut. 27:21) and punishable by death (Ex. 22:19; Lev. 20:15).

beth The second letter of the HEBREW alphabet.

Bezae See CODEX BEZAE.

biblical theology Doctrine as it is derived from the entire Bible. Biblical theology can also indicate doctrinal content derived from a portion of the Bible (e.g., Old Testament theology, Pauline theology, etc.). See also THEOLOGY.

bibliology Study of the Bible, its origin, character, and teachings.

bigamy   Marriage to two persons simultaneously; a form of polygamy.

birthright   According to Jewish custom, the rights and privileges enjoyed by the FIRSTBORN son, such as a double portion of the inheritance (Deut. 21:15–17). One's birthright was considered sacred, and its loss was disgraceful (Gen. 25:27–34; 49:3–7).

bishop   Traditional designation for a church leader responsible for supervising (Gk., *episkopos*, "one who oversees") people and affairs (Phil. 1:1; 1 Tim. 3:2; Titus 1:7). The term is used of Christ (1 Peter 2:25), of the apostolic office (Acts 1:20), and later of local church leaders (Phil. 1:1) whose qualifications, delineated in 1 Timothy 3:1–7 and Titus 1:7–9, include being above reproach, self-controlled, respectable, able to teach, and free from the love of money. Sometimes translated "overseer." See also OVERSEER.

B

black theology   A twentieth-century movement in the United States that sought to raise awareness of the distinct identity and experiences of black Christianity. Some have considered black theology a subcategory of "liberation theology," since release from oppression is a central theme. See also LIBERATION THEOLOGY.

blasphemy   Speaking evil, especially of God (Lev. 24:11; Ps. 74:18; Isa. 52:5; Rom. 2:24), but also of royalty (1 Kings 21:10) and others in general (Eph. 4:31; Col. 3:8; Titus 3:2). Blasphemy against God was punishable by stoning (Lev. 24:16). Jesus was accused of blasphemy (Matt. 9:3; Mark 14:64), and he himself called blasphemy of the Holy Spirit the UNFORGIVABLE SIN (Matt. 12:31; Mark 3:28–29).

blessing   Good fortune, or a statement or prayer about good fortune; the opposite of a CURSE (Gen. 27:12; Deut. 11:26–29; James 3:10). In the Old Testament blessings are often material

(Prov. 10:22). In the New Testament they are often spiritual advantages conferred by God (Eph. 1:3–14).

bondservant   A servant or slave (Gk., *doulos*, "slave"). The term often appears in New Testament prescripts (Rom. 1:1; Phil. 1:1; Titus 1:1; James 1:1; Rev. 1:1) designating a subordinate position and often suggesting allegiance and permanent servitude, especially to God (see also Matt. 8:9; 20:27; Gal. 1:10).

B

Book of the Twelve   See TWELVE, BOOK OF THE.

born again   The state that results from becoming a child of God (John 1:13; 1 Peter 1:23). Jesus contrasts spiritual birth with physical birth in John 3:1–7. See also REGENERATION.

boustrophedon   A style of writing that proceeds from right to left on one line, then left to right on the next line, then right to left on the next line, and so forth (Gk., "[as] an ox turns [when plowing]").

brazen serpent   See BRONZE SERPENT.

bread of the Presence   UNLEAVENED BREAD placed on a table in the TABERNACLE (see Ex. 25:23–30) to represent the presence of YAHWEH (Lev. 24:5–9; 1 Chron. 23:29). Every SABBATH twelve new loaves replaced the old ones, which, except in the case of David and his hungry men in 1 Samuel 21:4–6, were eaten only by the priests. Also known as shewbread or showbread.

breastpiece   A small nine-by-nine-inch pouch decorated with twelve gems (which were inscribed with the names of the tribes of ISRAEL) attached to the HIGH PRIEST's tunic that held the URIM AND THUMMIM, which were used in making decisions (see Ex. 28:15–30; 39:8–21; Lev. 8:8).

breastplate   A metal shield wielded in one hand by Roman soldiers to protect the chest, lungs, and heart. Paul draws on this imagery (the "breastplate of righteousness," Eph. 6:14) in a discussion of believers' battles with and defense against SATAN.

bride of Christ   A term for the CHURCH, derived from the biblical image of Christ's marriage to the church (2 Cor. 11:2; Eph. 5:24–27; Rev. 19:7–9; 21:2).

brimstone   Sulfuric material found in the valley of the Dead Sea and in other regions of volcanic activity that is occasionally spoken of in passages about divine punishment (Job 18:15; Isa. 34:9). Many of these texts make reference to "fire" (Gen. 19:24; Ps. 11:6; Ezek. 38:22; Rev. 21:8).

Bronze Age   The era from roughly 3000 to 1200 B.C.E.

bronze serpent   An IMAGE of a snake fashioned by Moses and placed high on a pole. The Israelites were commanded to look at the image, which enabled them to survive the attack of poisonous snakes sent by God to punish them for their complaining (Num. 21:4–9). In John 3:14–15, Jesus compares himself to this snake, inviting people to look to him as he is lifted up (the CRUCIFIXION) so they may receive eternal life. Also called brazen serpent. See also TYPOLOGICAL INTERPRETATION.

burnt offering   A SACRIFICE prescribed by the MOSAIC LAW, in which a bull, ram, or male bird was burned completely (see HOLOCAUST) in order to atone for an individual's unintentional sins (Lev. 1:1–17). One of five offerings described in Leviticus, including the GRAIN OFFERING, PEACE OFFERING, SIN OFFERING, and GUILT OFFERING.

Byzantine text-type   A late form of the New Testament text that originated in the Byzantine Empire and is characterized by textual additions and simplification of complicated passages. As the New Testament was copied and recopied, three distinct forms of the text, named for their supposed place of origin, developed: Byzantine, Western, and Alexandrian. The majority of existing manuscripts, mostly late and including the RECEIVED TEXT, represent the Byzantine text-type. Also known as the Syrian or Koine text-type. See also ALEXANDRIAN TEXT-TYPE and WESTERN TEXT-TYPE.

B

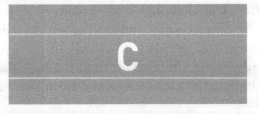

C.E. See A.D.

caesar The title, in keeping with the surname of Gaius Julius Caesar (100–44 B.C.E.), given to the line of Roman emperors from Octavian (63 B.C.E.–14 C.E.) until the death of Nero (37–68 C.E.). Three caesars are mentioned by name in the New Testament: Octavian or Augustus (Luke 2:1), Tiberius (Luke 3:1), and Claudius (Acts 11:28; 18:2).

Cairo Codex A Hebrew MANUSCRIPT (also called Codex Cairensis) dating from around 895 C.E. that contains all of the Old Testament prophets (both FORMER PROPHETS and LATTER PROPHETS). Represented by the siglum "C."

Cairo Prophets See CAIRO CODEX.

call, calling God's choice of an individual or nation. In the Old Testament, prophets are often called into their profession (1 Sam. 3:4–10; Jer. 1:4–10). In the New Testament, Christians are called to become children of God (Rom. 8:30; Eph. 4:1, 4).

Calvary The hill where Christ was crucified, thought to resemble a human skull (Lat., "skull"; see Luke 23:33). Others have suggested that the name reflects the multiplicity of executions at that location or the large number of skulls found there. See also GOLGOTHA.

Calvinism The doctrines and teachings of John Calvin (1509–1564), his successors, and the Reformed tradition generally. Sometimes the term is used strictly of the five points of Calvinism (developed after Calvin's death), or specifically of PREDESTINATION, LIMITED ATONEMENT, and so on. See TULIP.

Calvinism, five points of A summary of the doctrines emphasized by John Calvin's followers, articulated in this way only after his death. The five points of CALVINISM are: 1) TOTAL DEPRAVITY, 2) UNCONDITIONAL ELECTION, 3) LIMITED ATONEMENT, 4) IRRESISTIBLE GRACE, and 5) PERSEVERANCE OF THE SAINTS.

Canaan Another name for PALESTINE, occupied by the descendants of Canaan, the son of Ham and grandson of Noah (Gen. 9:18). The occupants of Canaan were at odds with the Israelites from the time of Joshua.

canon A rule or law, originally used of a measuring instrument in the sense of a standard (Gk., "reed"). Commonly refers to the list of books that collectively constitute Scripture (*the* canon); likewise the term can be used in a restricted sense, as in OLD TESTAMENT canon and NEW TESTAMENT canon. The term "closed canon" (or "fixed canon") refers to the theological concept that inspired Scripture ceased to be written at the end of the APOSTOLIC AGE. In biblical studies, the term can also refer to church rules or to principles followed by COPYISTS of MANUSCRIPTS (canons of TEXTUAL CRITICISM), and so on.

canonical gospel A gospel included in the Bible: Matthew, Mark, Luke, or John.

canonical prophet A book in the Bible containing the prophecies of a PROPHET and bearing his name (e.g., Isaiah, Amos, and Jonah).

canopy theory   The theory that the antediluvian earth was enveloped by a canvas of moisture (see Gen. 1:6–8), creating "greenhouse" conditions that account for the remarkable longevity of people described in Genesis 5. This theory proposes that the first occurrence of rain was that which led to the GENESIS FLOOD.

Cantabrigiensis   See CODEX BEZAE.

Canticles   Latinized name of the Song of Songs or Song of Solomon, from the Latin VULGATE title, *Canticum Canticorum*.

C

Cappadocian Fathers   Basil of Caesarea ("Basil the Great"; c. 330–379), Gregory of Nazianzus ("Gregory the Theologian"; c. 329–389), and Gregory of Nyssa (c. 330–395), Cappadocians by birth, whose philosophic arguments proved instrumental in defeating ARIANISM at the Council of Constantinople in 381 C.E. Also known as the "Great Cappadocians." Cappadocia is an area of Asia Minor (see Acts 2:9 and 1 Peter 1:1).

capstone   The top stone in a structure, especially of an archway. The New Testament quotes Psalm 118:22 as a reference to Christ (Mark 12:10; Acts 4:11).

carbon dating   A method for determining the approximate date of ancient organic materials, such as bone, wood, and PAPYRUS and PARCHMENT manuscripts. Also called radiocarbon dating or carbon 14.

carnal   Pertaining to flesh (Lat., *carnalis*, "flesh"). In theology, carnality denotes desires and behavior that are worldly or sensual, and the carnal Christian is one who follows his or her sinful desires (1 Cor. 3:1–3). See also FLESH.

case   The feature of the NOUN whereby its relationship to other words is indicated (e.g., whether a word is functioning as the subject or the object). In Hebrew, case is indicated by context and word order; in Greek it is indicated by form (i.e., declensions).

casemate walls A double wall system surrounding a city for added fortification. The walls were separated by a narrow corridor and were relatively thin, normally composed of stone or brick.

cataphatic theology A theological approach that describes God positively ("affirmation") on the basis of his self-revelation, as opposed to APOPHATIC THEOLOGY, which describes God negatively. Also called POSITIVE THEOLOGY.

C

catechism Oral or written instruction in the Christian faith often given in preparation for BAPTISM or first COMMUNION (Gk., *katechizein*, "to make hear").

catechumen In the early church, one receiving oral or written instruction in preparation for Christian BAPTISM (Gk., *katechoumenos*, "one who hears").

catholic In its broader sense, universal or general in nature. "Catholic church" refers to the UNIVERSAL CHURCH, though the term often appears as shorthand for the later Roman Catholic Church.

Catholic Epistles James, 1 and 2 Peter, 1, 2, and 3 John, and Jude. These general letters ("catholic" means general or universal), bearing the names of their presumed authors, were written for a broad Christian readership and not, as most New Testament letters, to an individual or local assembly (2 and 3 John are exceptions). Also known as General Epistles.

Catholicism The Roman Catholic Church or its teachings, history, and so on.

censer A portable, bowl-shaped vessel designed to carry hot coals for burning incense (Lev. 16:12), made either of bronze (Num. 16:6–7, 39) or gold (1 Kings 7:50).

centurion A high-ranking officer in the Roman army who served as commander of a hundred soldiers (Lat., *centum*, "one hundred"). Some centurions in the New Testament are sympathetic to the message of Christ (Matt. 8:5–13; Luke 23:47; Acts 10:1–11:18).

ceremonial law According to COVENANT THEOLOGY, the division of the MOSAIC LAW that deals with sacrifices, ritual purification, and other areas fulfilled in Christ (Heb. 9–10). Thus many believe that Christians are exempt from the Old Testament ceremonial law. See also CIVIL LAW and MORAL LAW.

ceremonially unclean According to MOSAIC LAW, the state of being profane and in need of ritual purification, which would often cut a person off from social privileges for a period of time. This state could be brought about by, among other things, a sexual discharge (Lev. 15:16–33), childbirth (Lev. 12:4–8), contact with the dead (Lev. 11:24–40; 17:15), or leprosy (Lev. 13–14). Ceremonial purification could usually be accomplished—after the prescribed period of waiting—by washing in water and/or sacrificing a year-old lamb or two turtledoves or pigeons (cf. Luke 2:23–24). Also, certain animals are said to be unclean, defiling anyone who eats them (Lev. 11:4–31). Certain practices and foods that would have rendered someone unclean in the Old Testament seem to be acceptable in the New Testament (Mark 7:15–22; Acts 10:14–15; 1 Cor. 8:8; 1 Tim. 4:3–5). Sometimes simply "unclean" or "defiled."

cessationism The belief that certain spiritual gifts, usually PROPHECY, healing, and SPEAKING IN TONGUES, are no longer granted to believers or operative in the life of the church. Most cessationists argue that these gifts were necessary during the infancy of the church but died out at the close of the first century with the death of the apostles. See also APOSTOLIC AGE.

Chalcedonian   Pertaining to the conclusions of the Council of Chalcedon in 451 C.E., which produced a definition of faith stating that Christ was fully human and fully God, manifested in two natures (from Chalcedon, an ancient city in Asia Minor).

Chaldea   A southern Babylonian territory (see Ezek. 23:15, 23) whose inhabitants were known for their ferocity in warfare (Job 1:17). Often the term denotes Babylonia as a whole. Furthermore, the term "Chaldean" was used technically for astrologers and wise men (e.g., Dan. 5:7, 11, where it is translated "astrologers").

chariot of fire   The supernatural vehicle that appeared suddenly to carry Elijah to heaven (2 Kings 2:11).

charis   A Greek term meaning "grace."

charisma   Transliteration of the Greek word for "gift," especially spiritual gifts (Rom. 12:6–8; 1 Cor. 12:8–11; Eph. 4:11). "Charismatic" often describes Christians or denominations that place particular emphasis on spiritual gifts, especially those of healing, PROPHECY, and SPEAKING IN TONGUES. Also known as charisms.

charismatic gifts   Spiritual gifts (Gk., *charismata*, "gifts"). See SIGN GIFTS.

Chassidim   See HASIDIM.

cheap grace   See LORDSHIP SALVATION.

cherubim   Heavenly creatures with four faces and four wings each (Ezek. 10:14, 21), who guarded the entrance to the Garden

48

of Eden (Gen. 3:24) and whose replica were placed on the ARK of the covenant (Ex. 25:18–22; Num. 7:89). TABERNACLE curtains were embroidered with their images (Ex. 26:1), and large statues of them were placed prominently in the Most Holy Place of SOLOMON'S TEMPLE (1 Kings 6:23–28). They are sometimes associated with divine transportation (2 Sam. 22:11; Ezek. 10:18–22). Plural of cherub; also called cherubs or, incorrectly, cherubims.

Chester Beatty Papyri   A valuable and diverse collection of PAPYRUS manuscripts written in Greek, many of substantial length, acquired in 1931 by A. Chester Beatty of London and comprised primarily of Old and New Testament selections dating from the second to the fourth century.

chiasm   A literary device in which words or ideas are stated and then restated in inverted order following an A-B-B-A pattern (e.g., Ps. 22:8) or an A-B-C-B-A pattern in which "C" is emphatic (e.g., Jonah 1:4–16). In this latter passage Jonah's CONFESSION in verse 9 is the central thought. Also called inverted parallelism.

chief priests   Members of the high-priestly families who served in the SANHEDRIN, the Jewish governing body of the first century. These, in league with scribes, elders, and Pharisees, are antagonistic toward Christ in the Gospels (Matt. 21:15, 23, 45–46; Mark 14:1; 15:10–11; Luke 9:22; 22:2; John 11:47; 18:3). Also called high priests.

chiliasm   The view, held by PREMILLENNIALISTS, that Christ will return to establish an earthly paradise, the millennial kingdom (Gk., *chilias*, "thousand"). Some in the early church held to a form of chiliasm; however, it died out soon after Augustine (354–430) propagated the idea that the MILLENNIUM is not a literal one-thousand-year period but the era from Christ's ASCENSION to his SECOND COMING. Also called millennialism.

chosen people A nation or community especially incorporated into the redemptive plan of God at a given time. In the Old Testament, ISRAEL (Ex. 19:3–6; Isa. 44:1); in the New Testament, the CHURCH (Col. 3:12; 1 Peter 2:9–10).

Christ Transliteration of the Greek word *Christos,* meaning "anointed one." This word bears the same meaning as the Hebrew *Mashiach* (see MESSIAH). In the New Testament, the title is reserved exclusively for Jesus of Nazareth, apart from the mention of "false Christs" (Matt. 24:24; Mark 13:22).

C

Christian One who belongs to Christ. The term may have first been used pejoratively by opponents ("The disciples were called Christians first at Antioch"; Acts 11:26; see also 26:28), but Christians apparently embraced the title (1 Peter 4:16).

Christmas Annual commemoration of the birth of Jesus celebrated on December 25; or the birth itself.

Christology The study of the nature and person of JESUS CHRIST—before, during, and since his INCARNATION. Christological topics include his DEITY, his humanity, his work on the cross, his place in the TRINITY, and his current ministry at the right hand of the Father.

Chronicler The alleged author or compiler of 1–2 Chronicles, Ezra, and Nehemiah. Some have conjectured that Ezra was the Chronicler.

chronos Greek for time, meaning "chronological time."

church In the New Testament, a local assembly of believers (e.g., the church at Thessalonica, 1 Thess. 1:1) that normally met in someone's house (1 Cor. 16:19). Also may denote all Christians from all time (see Eph. 1:22; 5:23; Heb. 12:23). See also UNIVERSAL CHURCH.

OF BIBLE AND THEOLOGY WORDS

church age   The present time, from the establishment of the church on the Day of PENTECOST (Acts 2:1–4) until the future return of Christ.

church father   See PATRISTIC ERA.

circumcision   The cutting away of the foreskin of the penis, usually that of an infant. This procedure, still widely performed today, was prescribed in connection with the ABRAHAMIC COVENANT (Gen. 17:10–14) and became the outward sign that the Israelites were God's CHOSEN PEOPLE. Occasionally the concept of circumcision of the heart appears in Scripture, picturing one's relationship with God as not only external but, more importantly, internal (Deut. 30:6; Jer. 4:4; Rom. 2:28–29).

circumlocution   Communication with indirect language or roundabout speech. For example, Jeremiah 17:16 literally reads "before your face," a circumlocution for God himself. Also known as periphrasis.

circumstantial   Pertaining to a PARTICIPLE or CLAUSE that provides the circumstances surrounding the action of the main VERB being modified.

civil law   According to COVENANT THEOLOGY, the division of the MOSAIC LAW that served to govern national Israel, in which God functioned as their king (e.g., Ex. 22). Thus many believe that Christians are exempt from the Old Testament civil law. See also CEREMONIAL LAW and MORAL LAW.

clan   A cluster of households—normally composed of extended family members—living in close proximity for cultural, economic, or social reasons. The Hebrew nation was made up of tribes, which in turn were made up of clans, which in turn were made up of families.

classical apologetics The branch of APOLOGETICS that argues for the existence of God through logical and philosophical reasoning. Examples include the COSMOLOGICAL ARGUMENT, TELEOLOGICAL ARGUMENT, and ONTOLOGICAL ARGUMENT.

Classical Greek The GREEK language from Homer (eighth century B.C.E.) through Plato (fourth century B.C.E.), existing in three major dialects: Doric, Aeolic, and Ionic.

classical prophet A biblical PROPHET whose written prophecies bear his name. See also LATTER PROPHETS.

C

clause A dependent or independent sequence of words normally containing a SUBJECT and PREDICATE and found in a compound or complex sentence.

clean See CEREMONIALLY UNCLEAN.

clergy Those employed in vocational ministry, especially the local church.

climactic parallelism In Hebrew poetry, a literary device in which a thought or idea is stated in one line and then repeated and developed or extended in two or more subsequent lines leading up to a climactic statement (e.g., Ps. 29:1–2). Also known as step-parallelism.

codex A MANUSCRIPT in book form made by folding PAPYRUS (plant) or PARCHMENT (animal skin) sheets in half and then sewing together the seams. Codices date from the late first or early second century C.E. when they began to replace scrolls as standard writing material. Codices can hold a large number of leafs with writing on both sides; thus they were not only easier to handle than scrolls, but they could also hold more text. The vast majority of New Testament manuscripts are codices (plural of codex) or sheets from codices. It is the precursor of the modern-day book (Lat., *codex*, "book").

Codex Aleppo   A Hebrew MANUSCRIPT dating from about 925 C.E. that contains most of the Hebrew Bible, though most of the PENTATEUCH is no longer extant. Represented by the siglum "A."

Codex Alexandrinus   A fifth-century Greek MANUSCRIPT of almost the entire Bible, including the APOCRYPHA and some other books. It is especially important for New Testament TEXTUAL CRITICISM. It is representative of the BYZANTINE TEXT-TYPE in the Gospels and the ALEXANDRIAN TEXT-TYPE in Acts and the Epistles. It has one of the best preserved texts of the book of Revelation. This codex, currently housed in the British Museum, is also denoted by "A" and "02."

Codex Claromontanus   A sixth-century MANUSCRIPT in Greek and Latin that contains all of Paul's letters, plus Hebrews, as well as some NONCANONICAL books.

Codex Bezae   A fourth- or fifth-century Greek and Latin MANUSCRIPT containing most of the four Gospels (in this order: Matthew, John, Luke, and Mark), Acts, and a fragment of 3 John. This codex, named after Theodore Beza, who presented it to the library at Cambridge University (where it remains today), is nearly one-tenth longer in the book of Acts than the text generally received. It is the principal representative of the so-called WESTERN TEXT-TYPE. Also known as Cantabrigiensis and denoted by "D" and "05."

Codex Cairo   See CAIRO CODEX.

Codex Cantabrigiensis   See CODEX BEZAE.

Codex Ephraemi   A fifth-century Greek MANUSCRIPT of relatively small selections of the Old Testament and a little more than half the New Testament. In the twelfth century the original writing was erased so that the parchment could be reused (a manuscript of this sort is called a PALIMPSEST), but through various methods paleographers are able to read the underlying biblical text.

Codex Leningrad   A Hebrew MANUSCRIPT dating from 1008 C.E. that contains the entire Hebrew Bible. This codex preserves the MASORETIC TEXT and was the basis for the printed Hebrew text *Biblia Hebraica Stuttgartensia*, third edition. Represented by the siglum "L."

C

Codex Petersburg   See PETERSBURG CODEX.

Codex Sinaiticus   A fourth-century Greek MANUSCRIPT containing most of the Old Testament, the entire New Testament, as well as some NONCANONICAL books. Discovered in the middle of the nineteenth century at the monastery of St. Catherine at Mount Sinai, it is perhaps the single most important extant New Testament manuscript, generally representing the ALEXANDRIAN TEXT-TYPE. Denoted by "א" and "01."

Codex Vaticanus   A fourth-century Greek MANUSCRIPT of almost the entire Bible, as well as most of the books of the APOCRYPHA. This New Testament manuscript reflects the ALEXANDRIAN TEXT-TYPE. Denoted by "B" and "03."

Codex Washingtonensis   A late fourth- or early fifth-century Greek MANUSCRIPT of the GOSPELS. It is the earliest manuscript to contain the Gospels in the so-called Western order: Matthew, John, Luke, and Mark. Also known as Freerianus and Washingtoniansus.

codices   Plural of CODEX.

cognate   In language study, a word that shares the same ROOT with another word (e.g., "holy" and "holiness"), or a word that is borrowed from another language (e.g., the English word *wine* is cognate to the Greek *oinos*, which in turn is cognate to the Hebrew *yayin*). Related languages are also referred to as cognate languages. See also LOANWORD.

cohortative   In Hebrew, an imperfect verb in the first person that conveys desire or intention. For example, following Ezra's rebuke regarding intermarriage among the Israelites, a spokesperson expresses the desire and intention of the people: "*Let us make a covenant* before our God to send away all these women and their children" (Ezra 10:3).

Comma Johanneum   A phrase used to denote 1 John 5:7–8 in the BYZANTINE TEXT-TYPE. This dubious portion of text probably originated in Jerome's fourth-century VULGATE and gained credibility in the sixteenth century when Erasmus included it in the third edition of his Greek New Testament. The oldest and best witnesses show no trace of this passage.

commercial theory of the atonement   See SATISFACTION THEORY OF THE ATONEMENT.

common era   Abbreviated C.E. See A.D.

common grace   The kindness of God extended to humankind in restraining evil and promoting good. Such grace is "common" to all humanity, believers and unbelievers (see Matt. 5:45).

Communion   The church SACRAMENT commemorating the so-called "LAST SUPPER" (Matt. 26:17–30; Mark 14:12–26; Luke 22:7–23), in which a small amount of bread and wine (or grape juice) is consumed by participants in memory of the body and blood of the crucified Christ (1 Cor. 11:23–26). Also called Holy Communion, the Lord's Supper, or EUCHARIST.

comparative degree   Feature of adjectives and adverbs to denote relative difference in intensity, quality, quantity, and so on, as in "greater" in John 8:53: "Are you greater than our father Abraham?" This is in contrast to POSITIVE DEGREE and SUPERLATIVE DEGREE.

comparative parallelism   In Hebrew poetry, a literary device in which a simile or metaphor explains or develops a principle or thought (Ps. 103:13). Also known as emblematic PARALLELISM.

concentric structuring   See CHIASM.

concordance   A book that lists biblical words alphabetically and where they occur in the text.

concubine   A woman legally married to a man yet holding an inferior position to his wife or wives. Concubines are mentioned often in the Old Testament (e.g., Gen. 22:24; Judg. 19:1; 2 Sam. 3:7). They were either purchased (or exchanged for gifts) or acquired by military victory.

conditional sentence   A sentence containing an "if-then" construction, in which an inference, result, or statement of fact in the APODOSIS (the "then" statement) is contingent upon the PROTASIS (the "if" statement).

conditioned immortality   See ANNIHILATIONISM.

confession   A proclamation of truth, usually in the form of praise (1 Kings 8:35), repentance (1 John 1:9), or conversion (Rom. 10:9), or an elaborate statement of a denomination's THEOLOGY (e.g., The Westminster Confession and The Augsburg Confession).

conjectural emendation   In TEXTUAL CRITICISM, the reconstruction of the original wording of a biblical passage by inferring what it might have said rather than choosing from among the existing readings of manuscripts (Lat., *emendare*, "remove faults"). See also EMENDATION.

conjunction   A word that connects (Lat., "join together") words, phrases, clauses, sentences, or paragraphs. Conjunctions are often significant for exegesis, variously denoting subordination, contrast, summation, continuation, and so on.

consecrate   To set aside something or someone for the service or worship of God. Among items consecrated in the Old Testament were Levites (Ex. 32:28–29), vessels (Lev. 8:11), Israel (Ex. 19:6, 10), and animals (2 Chron. 29:33).

consort   The spouse of a god or reigning king.

construct state   In Hebrew, the condition of a NOUN that is so closely linked to the following word that they are counted together, and whose translation usually requires the English PREPOSITION "of" (e.g., "sweat" in "sweat of your brow," Gen. 3:19, is in the construct state). See also ABSOLUTE STATE.

consubstantiation   The belief, often associated with Martin Luther, that the physical body and blood of Christ abide together with the elements during COMMUNION (lit., "with substance"). This represents a middle position between TRANSUBSTANTIATION, in which the elements are entirely replaced by the body and blood of Christ, and the MEMORIAL VIEW OF COMMUNION, in which the elements remain unchanged.

continuous parallelism   In Hebrew poetry, a literary device in which a thought or idea is stated in one line and then repeated and further developed in the next line (Ps. 95:3). See also SYNTHETIC PARALLELISM.

Coptic A form of the Egyptian language composed primarily of the Greek alphabet and important for TEXTUAL CRITICISM. The New Testament was translated into Coptic by the fourth century; the SEPTUAGINT was translated soon after.

corban An offering intended for God (Heb., *qorban*, "offering"), usually in fulfillment of a vow (see Mark 7:11).

cornerstone The first and most important stone laid in the foundation of a structure, to which all other stones are aligned to ensure structural stability. Used both literally of building construction (Job 38:6) and figuratively of important people (Isa. 19:13), especially Christ (e.g., Eph. 2:20; 1 Peter 2:5–7).

cosmological argument An argument for the existence of God that states that since the universe and everything in it exists and is governed by causation, there must be an "uncaused Cause" or "unmoved Mover" (i.e., God). Also known as the argument from causation. See also CLASSICAL APOLOGETICS.

cosmos Transliteration of the Greek word for "arrangement" or "system," variously denoting the earth (Matt. 13:35; Acts 17:24), humankind (Matt. 5:14; John 1:9), or the present system of human affairs (1 Cor. 2:12; Gal. 4:3; 1 John 4:5). The term appears frequently in John's writings, normally suggesting a universe or system hostile to Christ and his followers (John 7:7; 8:23; 12:19; 14:27; 18:36; 1 John 4:4; 5:18–19) and over which Christ experiences victory (John 3:16–17; 8:12; 16:33).

court of the Gentiles See GENTILE COURT.

covenant A promise or binding agreement between two or more parties; a contract (e.g., ABRAHAMIC COVENANT, MOSAIC COVENANT). Ancient Near Eastern covenants often involved obligations as well as the guarantee of blessings for faithfulness and consequences for unfaithfulness (see Deut. 28–29). The author of Hebrews claims that the covenant established by Jesus is superior to the old covenant, the MOSAIC LAW (Heb. 7:22; 8:6). See also COVENANT OF GRANT, SUZERAIN-VASSAL COVENANT, and PARITY COVENANT.

covenant of grant An unconditional grant of land or dynastic status issued by a powerful king (suzerain) to a person in reward for past loyalty. Because of that loyalty, there was no further obligation stipulated on the part of the vassal. Moreover, anyone who violated the vassal's newly granted rights faced the wrath of the suzerain. God's covenants with Abraham and David are often cited as this type of covenant. See also PARITY COVENANT and SUZERAIN-VASSAL COVENANT.

covenant theology A theological system that emphasizes the biblical covenants, especially the covenants of works and grace (Gal. 4:24–31). Occasionally used interchangeably with REFORMED THEOLOGY.

covet To desire the life or property of someone else. The tenth commandment forbids coveting (Ex. 20:17). See also TEN COMMANDMENTS.

crasis The blending of two words into one new word. In the Greek New Testament, crasis only occurs when the first of the two words is the neuter article or the conjunction "and."

creationism The belief that God made the world and everything in it, as opposed to EVOLUTION, PANTHEISM, DUALISM, and so on. In THEOLOGY, the term can also refer to the view that God creates each person's SOUL at the moment of conception, as opposed to TRADUCIANISM, which asserts that human souls are propagated by parents.

creed A succinct statement of doctrine, such as the APOSTLES' CREED and the NICENE CREED.

crisis theology See DIALECTICAL THEOLOGY.

critical apparatus In TEXTUAL CRITICISM, the body of footnotes in printed editions of the Hebrew Scriptures or the Greek New Testament that provides the MANUSCRIPT evidence for that edition's biblical text and significant VARIANT readings.

critical scholar In biblical and theological studies, one who uses scientific means of historical and critical inquiry to investigate the Bible and the Christian tradition (especially issues pertaining to backgrounds, sources, HISTORICITY, AUTHORSHIP, message, social function, etc.).

cross See CRUCIFIXION.

cross-reference A biblical reference in the margin or center column of some Bibles that directs readers to other biblical passages that are somehow related to the original passage. The term can also be used as a verb (i.e., to "cross-reference" a passage).

crucifixion The tying or nailing of a convicted criminal to a cross for the purpose of public humiliation and execution. Usually the victim would remain alive for more than a day before dying of asphyxiation or, less likely, loss of blood. Crucifixion was practiced by many ancient cultures; it became a standard method of execution in the Roman Empire.

cult The established religious practices of a people, including rites, rituals, festivals and holy days, the veneration of certain sites, and so on. The term is also used popularly as a synonym for "sect," especially a religious group considered aberrant. Also, the term appears in some English translations of certain Old Testament passages with reference to groups that practiced IDOLATRY and PAGAN worship (Deut. 23:17; 1 Kings 14:24; 15:12; "shrine" in the NIV). Participation in cult prostitution and other pagan cultic practices (e.g., human sacrifice) is expressly forbidden in the Old Testament (Lev. 18; Deut. 12:29–32).

cuneiform   Writing composed of wedge-shaped characters (Lat., *cuneus*, "wedge") employed in ancient ASSYRIA, BABYLONIA, and PERSIA, among other nations.

cupbearer   A trusted, high-ranking palace official in the courts of the ANCIENT NEAR EAST, who was obligated personally to deliver and, on occasion, to taste the king's beverages (e.g., Neh. 1:11).

C

curse   Punishment for disobedience (Gen. 3:14–15), usually disobedience to the Mosaic covenant (Deut. 11:26–28; 28:16–68); the opposite of BLESSING. In the New Testament, Christ is said to redeem believers from the curse brought on them by the MOSAIC LAW because of their inability to keep it perfectly (Gal. 3:10–13). More generally, the term means "to denounce verbally" (Prov. 11:26; James 3:9).

cursive   An informal style of writing employed in the production of everyday documents and characterized by contractions and abbreviations, or a MANUSCRIPT containing such writing. Cursive writing was rapid, not requiring the pen to leave the paper (Lat., *cursus*, "run"). The vast majority of New Testament Greek manuscripts are cursives dating from the ninth to the fifteenth century. Also referred to as a "running hand."

D   According to the DOCUMENTARY HYPOTHESIS, the "Deuteronomist" source in the PENTATEUCH, which essentially constitutes the book of Deuteronomy.

dagesh   In Hebrew, a dot within a consonant indicating either an alternative pronunciation (i.e., *dagesh lene,* "weak") or doubling of the consonant (i.e., *dagesh forte,* "strong").

Dagon   A principal Philistine grain deity (Heb., *dagan,* "grain"), whose image was decapitated when the ark of God was placed in its temple in Ashdod (1 Sam. 5:2–7; see also 1 Chron. 10:10). The name Dagan, presumably a cognate of "Dagon," is attested outside of the Bible in ancient Mesopotamian and Palestinian regions.

Dan to Beersheba   An Old Testament MERISM in which two cities in Israel are mentioned (Dan to the far north and Beersheba to the far south), but the entire nation is in mind.

dative   In Greek, the CASE that normally marks a word as the indirect object of the verb.

Davidic covenant   God's pledge to David that he would never lack a descendant on his throne (2 Sam. 7:8–17; see also Pss. 2; 110). Many regard the COVENANT as a promise that the MESSIAH would come through David's line. See also COVENANT OF GRANT.

63

Day of Atonement A religious holiday observed on the tenth of Tishri (September/October), during which Israel's HIGH PRIEST offered a SACRIFICE to atone for the nation's sin (Ex. 30:10; Lev. 16; 23:26–31; Num. 29:7–11). No work was to be done on this day (Heb., "Yom Kippur," lit., "Day of ATONEMENT").

Day of the LORD In ESCHATOLOGY, the future period when God will judge unbelievers. In the Old Testament, the term indicates punishment on Israel (Joel 1:15; Zeph. 1:7, 14) or some other specific nation (e.g., Egypt in Jer. 46:10) or humankind generally (Joel 2:31). In the New Testament, the Day of the Lord refers to the second coming of Christ (1 Cor. 1:8). Sometimes called simply "that day" or "the day" (2 Tim. 1:12, 18).

D

day-age theory A view of creation that understands "day" in Genesis 1 as an era or geological age rather than strictly a twenty-four-hour period. Day-age theorists are thus ostensibly able to reconcile the biblical account of creation with fossil records. Also called age-day theory.

deacon From a Greek term meaning "servant" (*diakonos*), whether an employee (Matt. 22:13; John 2:5, 9) or one who serves Christ (Col. 1:7). Also an office in the early church, whose responsibilities are unclear, although deacons probably assisted with the church's material needs (Acts 6:1–6; 1 Tim. 3:8–13). In Romans 15:8, Jesus is called "a servant [deacon] of the Jews."

deaconess A female servant of the Lord (Rom. 16:1). Paul's list of qualifications for women during his discussion of deacons (1 Tim. 3:8–13) has led some to conclude that deaconesses likewise had a leadership role in the early church. Others believe Paul listed qualities that should be true of the wives of deacons. See also DEACON.

Dead Sea Scrolls A collection of manuscripts dating from the second century B.C.E. to the first century C.E. first discovered in 1947 in caves at QUMRAN near the northwestern shore of the Dead Sea. Copies of every Old Testament book except Esther were found, along with several manuals pertaining to the life and conduct of the community (likely the ESSENES) that collected them.

debauchery Wastefulness commonly associated with an immoral lifestyle (Rom. 13:13; Gal. 5:19; 1 Peter 4:3).

Decalogue The TEN COMMANDMENTS (Gk., "ten words").

deism The belief, often traced to the seventeenth century, that while God created the world, he has by and large chosen not to participate in his creation. The deistic God is often termed the "Watchmaker," who built and wound the mechanical watch only to sit back and observe it run by its own power.

D

deity A god, God, or having all the qualities of God. Usually employed to speak of Christ's equality with the Father (i.e., the "deity of Christ").

Deluge See GENESIS FLOOD.

demon An ANGEL that has relinquished its holiness and favorable position with God (i.e., it has "fallen") as a result of sin. The New Testament describes some demons as imprisoned (Jude 6), while others are free to work evil (1 Tim. 4:1) and possess susceptible individuals (Luke 4:41). SATAN is called the chief of the demons (Matt. 12:24–27).

demoniac Someone possessed by a DEMON or demons as evidenced by their appearance or behavior.

demotic script An adaptation of Egyptian hieroglyphics popular from the seventh century B.C.E. until the fifth century C.E.

and characterized by abbreviations and efficient strokes (Gk., *demotikos*, "popular").

demythologization   A twentieth-century movement, normally associated with Rudolph Bultmann, to reinterpret the biblical text so as to discover the truths that lie behind its recorded MYTHS (e.g., MIRACLES, the INCARNATION, etc.). Demythologization thus attempted to make the Bible—and Christianity—more palatable for the modern, post-Enlightenment reader.

denarius   A unit of Roman currency probably equivalent to a day's wage (Matt. 20:1–16).

dependent clause   See SUBORDINATE CLAUSE.

deponent   In Greek, a verb in a MIDDLE (i.e., "deponent middle") or PASSIVE (i.e., "deponent passive") written form but with an ACTIVE meaning. A deponent verb is identifiable by its passive lexical form.

deportation   Forced physical separation from one's homeland. The term is most commonly used of the Babylonian exile of Judah occurring from 606/605 to 586 B.C.E. (2 Kings 25:21).

depravity   Humankind's natural condition as fallen, sinful, and completely incapable of earning God's favor (Rom. 1:28; 3:10–18). See also TOTAL DEPRAVITY.

descent into Hades   The belief that between the CRUCIFIXION and the RESURRECTION Jesus descended to the realm of the dead to proclaim the good news. Adherents look to 1 Peter 3:19 and 4:6 for support, and some versions of the APOSTLES' CREED include this "descent." Also called descent into Hell.

Designer   The intelligent architect (i.e., God) responsible for order in the world. The notion of Designer rests behind the TELEOLOGICAL ARGUMENT for the existence of God.

desolating sacrifice See ABOMINATION OF DESOLATION.

determinism In THEOLOGY, the belief that every thought and activity has been decided beforehand by God, thereby reducing or negating human responsibility. See also FREE WILL.

deuterocanonical See NONCANONICAL.

Deutero-Isaiah The name given by some to a presumed anonymous author of the second part of the book of Isaiah ("deutero" means "second") (chs. 40–66). Others believe a third author, "TRITO-ISAIAH," wrote chapters 56–66, in which case "Deutero-Isaiah" refers to Isaiah 40–55.

D

Deuteronomist document See D.

Deuteronomistic History Designation for the biblical books Deuteronomy through 2 Kings, which many scholars believe is the work of a single author or editor. These writings together present a unified history emphasizing the BLESSINGS and CURSES of the COVENANT as described particularly in Deuteronomy 27–28. Also Deuteronomic History.

deutero-Pauline epistles New Testament letters attributed to the apostle Paul but whose AUTHORSHIP is disputed: Ephesians, Colossians, 2 Thessalonians, and the PASTORAL EPISTLES.

devil A slanderer or accuser, most often used as a title for SATAN. The devil is described as the enemy of God and his people, and Christians are exhorted to stand firm against him (Eph. 6:11). He will one day be thrown into the lake of fire (Rev. 20:10).

diachronic Denoting change over time (Gk., "through time")—usually pertaining to words.

diadem   Transliteration of the Greek for a crown or head cloth worn by a king, usually Christ (Rev. 19:12), in contrast to a crown worn by men of honor but not of royalty (*stephanos*; 2 Tim. 4:8; Rev. 4:4, 10).

dialectical theology   A theological method (i.e., an approach to THEOLOGY and theological inquiry) associated with Karl Barth (1886–1968) and NEO-ORTHODOXY that emphasizes the paradoxical nature of theological truth. Thus theology can be expressed in terms of opposing pairs—grace and wrath, time and eternity, God and humanity, and so on. Moreover, God transcends rational thought; divine truth cannot be synthesized or articulated except by God-given faith. Also called crisis theology.

diaspora   Greek for "scattered abroad." See DISPERSION.

Diatessaron   A HARMONY of the four Gospels (Gk., *dia tessaron*, "through four") produced around 170 C.E. by Tatian. Also known as Tatian's Harmony.

dichotomism   The view that persons are made up of two parts: body and SOUL or SPIRIT. Some Christians look to God's use of dust (material) and breath (immaterial) in the creation of Adam as proof for dichotomism (Gen. 2:7; see also James 2:26). See also MONISM and TRICHOTOMISM.

dictation theory   A view of biblical INSPIRATION that claims that the exact words of the Bible were spoken directly to its writers by God.

Didache   A second-century Greek manual on local church protocol and Christian behavior (Gk., *didache*, "teaching"), whose author and place of origin are unknown. The *Didache*, also known as "The Teaching of the Twelve Apostles," is often included in the writings collectively called the APOSTOLIC FATHERS.

diglot   A bilingual book, such as one displaying the Greek New Testament on one side and an English TRANSLATION on the opposite side.

diphthong   The pronunciation of two juxtaposed vowels as one compound sound.

direct object   The NOUN or PRONOUN that receives the action of the verb.

dirge   A lamentation, often in the form of poetry or song, occasioned by someone's death or some other cause for sorrow or mourning (Lam. 1–4; Matt. 11:17; Luke 7:32).

D

disciple   A follower or student of a teacher (Lat., *discipulus,* "learner, student"). A disciple customarily embraces the views and practices of his or her teacher. In the Bible the term frequently refers to Jesus' TWELVE disciples (Matt. 10:1; 11:1), although it also designates other followers of Jesus (John 6:66; Acts 6:1–7), as well as students of Moses (John 9:28), John the Baptist (John 3:25), and the Pharisees (Mark 2:18), among others.

discourse analysis   Examination of a text at the paragraph or PERICOPE level. Thus, to determine a text's meaning, those who practice discourse analysis consider the development of a paragraph's clauses and sentences and how these contribute to the entire discourse.

dispensation   In THEOLOGY, God's management of humanity during a distinct age, or the age itself. For example, God dealt differently with Joshua's generation than he did with Joseph's, since Joseph lived before the giving of the MOSAIC LAW. The notion derives from a word (Gk., *oikonomia,* "house law," in some translations rendered "dispensation") that signifies a stewardship or administration of one's or another's affairs (Luke 16:2–4). See also DISPENSATIONALISM.

dispensationalism A method of interpreting Scripture that identifies successive stages (i.e., dispensations) in God's overall redemptive plan. Dispensationalism emphasizes a literal reading of the Scriptures, a clear separation between national ISRAEL and the CHURCH, and a future millennial kingdom in which Israel will receive blessings through Christ, her promised king. Traditionally seven dispensations have been recognized: ages of innocence, conscience or moral responsibility, human government, promise, the Law, grace or the church, and the MILLENNIUM, though some see fewer than seven. Dispensationalism is often traced to John Nelson Darby (1800–1882), though the early church held to a form of CHILIASM. See also DISPENSATION.

Dispersion Designation for Jewish settlements scattered throughout the ancient world following the BABYLONIAN CAPTIVITY (Est. 9:30; Zeph. 3:10; John 7:35). The Dispersion, or *diaspora* (Gk., "dispersion"), contributed to Jewish Hellenization and promoted SYNAGOGUE worship. Following the destruction of the temple in 70 C.E., the term was used of any Jews living outside of PALESTINE.

dissipation Wasteful consumption, often associated with indulging one's desires (Luke 21:34; 1 Peter 4:4).

dittography In TEXTUAL CRITICISM, the accidental duplication of material when copying a MANUSCRIPT (Gk., *dittos*, "double"). The opposite of HAPLOGRAPHY.

divided kingdom Name given to the Israelite nation following the 931 B.C.E. split (recorded in 1 Kings 12) into the SOUTHERN KINGDOM, JUDAH, which included the tribes of Judah and Benjamin, and the NORTHERN KINGDOM, ISRAEL, which included the remainder of the tribes. Also called the divided monarchy. See also UNITED KINGDOM.

divination Forecasting the future by employing PAGAN practices, such as astrology and necromancy; sorcery. Divination is expressly forbidden in the Old Testament (Lev. 19:26; Deut. 18:10).

divine name A reference to the name "YAHWEH" (Ex. 3:13–15).

divine oracle formula Any standardized expression introducing a message from God, such as "the LORD said to—" (1 Chron. 21:9) or "this is what the LORD says" (Isa. 45:1, 11, 14, 18; Jer. 29:4, 8, 10, 16, 17, 21, 25, 31, 32).

D

diviner One who forecasts the future by means such as astrology and necromancy; a sorcerer. See also DIVINATION.

docetism The belief that JESUS CHRIST only seemed to have a human body (Gk., *dokeo*, "to seem or appear") and only seemed to suffer and die. Teachings such as this that denied Jesus' humanity appeared early in the life of the church (see 1 John 4:1–3).

doctrine See THEOLOGY.

Documentary Hypothesis A theory used to explain the composition of the PENTATEUCH (the first five books of the Bible) as a compilation of four previously independent sources rather than the work of a single author (traditionally called "the five books of Moses"). These sources are referred to as J, E, D, and P, the order in which they were allegedly written. According to the theory, J refers to God as YAHWEH, E refers to God as ELOHIM, D constitutes the book of Deuteronomy, and P deals with priests and priestly duties.

dogma   An authoritative tenet or system of doctrine, sometimes used pejoratively of beliefs that are firmly held despite inadequate grounds. Plural, dogmas or dogmata.

dominical saying   A saying of Jesus (Lat., *dominus*, "lord").

Donatism   A fourth-century religious movement against those who wished to reenter the church assembly after denying their faith under persecution (called in Latin, *traditores*, "those who handed over"). Named after Donatus (d. 355 C.E.), a North African church leader.

D

double entendre   A word or expression that can be understood in two ways. For example, when the disciples of John the Baptist "followed" Jesus (John 1:37), they both walked with him and became his disciples.

double predestination   The belief that God not only selects individuals for eternal life but also chooses the remainder for eternal condemnation (see Rom. 9:18–22). Double predestination is commonly associated with CALVINISM. See also DETERMINISM.

dowry   A gift given by the groom or the groom's family to the father of the bride in exchange for marrying his daughter (Gen. 29:18; 34:12).

doxology   A short statement praising God (Gk., *doxa*, "glory," and *logos*, "word"), recited regularly in some churches (e.g., Ps. 147:1; Rom. 11:33–36). "The Doxology," denoting a popular expression of praise in Protestant churches taken from a HYMN by Thomas Ken, states, "Praise God from whom all blessings flow, praise him all creatures here below, praise him above ye heavenly hosts, praise Father, Son, and Holy Ghost."

drachma   A unit of Greek currency roughly equivalent to the Roman DENARIUS, which was about a day's wage (Luke 15:8).

OF BIBLE AND THEOLOGY WORDS

dragon A metaphorical designation for SATAN in the book of Revelation (especially chs. 12–13), probably denoting qualities associated with serpents, such as craftiness and deception (see 12:9; 20:2). The dragon gives power and authority to the beast, the ANTICHRIST (13:2, 4).

drink offering The pouring out of a drink, usually wine or oil, in ceremonial worship as prescribed by the MOSAIC LAW (Ex. 29:40–41; Num. 15:1–5). Drink offerings were to accompany grain, burnt, and peace offerings. In the New Testament, Paul speaks figuratively of his impending death as a drink offering (Phil. 2:17; 2 Tim. 4:6). Also called a libation.

D

dropsy Accumulation of fluids in bodily tissue, usually indicating a diseased organ (Gk., *hydropikos*, "full of water"). Luke 14:1–4 records Jesus' healing of a man with dropsy. Also known as ascites.

dual authorship A view of INSPIRATION that holds that each book of the Bible has both a divine author, giving the text absolute authority, and a human author, giving the text unique literary characteristics.

dualism The theological belief that the universe is made up of two relatively equal forces of good and evil, which eternally oppose one another. Or more generally, any twofold division in philosophy or THEOLOGY.

Dung Gate A city gate in the south wall of Jerusalem that led out to the Valley of Hinnom (i.e., GEHENNA), where refuse was disposed (Neh. 3:13–14; 12:31).

dynamic equivalence A TRANSLATION method that strives for readability over literalness in its rendering of the ORIGINAL text. Also called functional equivalence. See also FORMAL EQUIVALENCE.

dynamic monarchianism The belief traced to the early church that Jesus was a mere man through whom God powerfully worked during his public ministry.

dynasty A line of kings from the same family. In the Bible, the concept is normally associated with King David (1 Sam. 25:28), with implications that the MESSIAH would emerge from his never-ending line (Ps. 89:3–4, 29, 35–36; Luke 2:4).

D

E According to the DOCUMENTARY HYPOTHESIS, the "Elohist" source in the PENTATEUCH, so named for the frequent occurrence of the designation "ELOHIM" for God.

Early Bronze Age The era from 3000 to 2300 B.C.E.

Easter Annual commemoration of the resurrection of Jesus celebrated (in the West) on the first Sunday following the first full moon on or after March 21; or the resurrection itself.

easy believism See LORDSHIP SALVATION.

Ebionitism An early Jewish-Christian belief that Jesus was not divine but was a PROPHET chosen to be MESSIAH (Heb., *ebyon*, "a poor man," conveying their ASCETIC lifestyle). Jesus of Nazareth was said to be the human son of Joseph and Mary on whom the power of God rested from his BAPTISM until the end of his life. Also called Ebionism.

Ebla tablets A collection of approximately 18,000 texts dating from around 2300 B.C.E. discovered in 1964 at the ruins of the ancient city of Ebla. These writings provide cultural background for some of the early events of the Old Testament.

ecce homo Latin for "behold the man," the words spoken by Pilate concerning Jesus in John 19:5.

ecclesiology   The branch of THEOLOGY concerned with the study of the CHURCH (Gk., *ekklesia*, "assembly"), including its SACRAMENTS, offices, mission, and organization.

eclectic text   A printed edition of the Hebrew Scriptures or Greek New Testament that reflects a combination of the best readings from multiple manuscripts rather than relying solely on one MANUSCRIPT or TEXT-TYPE.

eclecticism   In TEXTUAL CRITICISM, any method that creates a text based on preferred readings from available manuscripts as opposed to giving preference entirely to one MANUSCRIPT or TEXT-TYPE. See also REASONED ECLECTICISM and RIGOROUS ECLECTICISM.

E

ecumenism   The pursuit of transdenominational unity in the church by focusing on common ground (Gk., *oikoumene*, "the inhabited world").

effectual call   In CALVINISM and the Reformed tradition, God's work of enlightening the elect as to their sinfulness and need of God's mercy in Christ, leading inevitably to their conversion (Rom. 8:30). According to some theologians, an effectual call is logically necessary because sin and spiritual blindness render humankind incapable of choosing God. Also called special calling. See also IRRESISTIBLE GRACE.

efficacy   The capability of bringing about a desired result. In THEOLOGY, efficacy usually denotes ability to secure SALVATION (e.g., the efficacy of the cross).

eight-case system   In GREEK, a method of classifying words that have CASE into eight cases (i.e., NOMINATIVE, ABLATIVE, GENITIVE, DATIVE, LOCATIVE, INSTRUMENTAL, ACCUSATIVE, and VOCATIVE), based on their function in a given context. This is in contrast to the FIVE-CASE SYSTEM, which classifies words based on their form.

eisegesis   The practice of imposing meaning on a text of Scripture (Gk., "to lead into") as opposed to EXEGESIS (Gk., "to lead out"), in which case the meaning is derived from the text.

ekklesia   A Greek term meaning "assembly," usually referring to the church. See also ECCLESIOLOGY.

El   A generic Hebrew designation for DEITY, which frequently appears in compound names for YAHWEH, such as El-Elyon ("God Most High"; Gen. 14:18–22), El-Shaddai ("God Almighty"; Gen. 17:1), and El-Roi ("the God who sees"; Gen. 16:13). El is also the designation of a prominent Canaanite deity. See also ELOHIM.

elder   An older man who has authority by virtue of his age and wisdom. In the Old Testament, seventy elders helped Moses lead Israel (Num. 11:16–30). In New Testament times, elders were influential members of the SANHEDRIN, the Jewish governing body (Mark 15:1). Christian elders were appointed to govern the church (Acts 14:23; Titus 1:5) if they met certain qualifications (1 Tim. 3:1–7; Titus 1:5–9).

elect   Those chosen by God for SALVATION, whether Israelites (Deut. 7:6) or Christians (1 Peter 1:1–2). See also ELECTION and UNCONDITIONAL ELECTION.

election   God's choosing for SALVATION a person or group of people from among fallen humanity (1 Thess. 1:4; 2 Peter 1:10). See also ELECT.

ellipsis   The omission of part of a sentence that is understood either from the context or from everyday vernacular. For example, the original Greek of Ephesians 5:22 does not contain a verb, but borrows it ("be subject") from the preceding verse.

Elohim   A generic Hebrew designation for DEITY, commonly referring to YAHWEH; plural of EL.

Elohist's narrative   See E.

embalming   An ancient Egyptian burial custom in which the body is prepared with oil and spices to prevent decomposition. Apparently Jacob and Joseph were embalmed (Gen. 50:2, 3, 26).

E

emblematic parallelism   See COMPARATIVE PARALLELISM.

emendation   Reconstruction of the original wording of the Bible, usually by identifying the copying errors that appear in the biblical manuscripts (Lat., *emendare*, "remove faults"). See also CONJECTURAL EMENDATION.

Emmanuel   See IMMANUEL.

emphatic position   The peculiar arrangement of a word or clause in a sentence that alerts the reader of its importance, usually by placing it at the beginning. For example, in John 12:46, the word "light" is brought forward in the sentence to emphasize that Jesus has come into the world *as a light* in order to dispel one's darkness.

Enuma Elish   An ancient Babylonian creation account in which the god MARDUK brings order out of chaos. The important role humankind plays in the Genesis creation account contrasts with that described in the *Enuma Elish*, according to which humans are created for the express purpose of serving the gods and reducing their workload.

1 Enoch   A collection of apocryphal Jewish traditions about Enoch (Gen. 5:18–24), containing five sections. This document was originally written in the second century B.C.E. (probably in Aramaic), and fragments of manuscript copies were discovered at Qumran.

ephah   A large vessel used for carrying cereals (Isa. 5:10), with the capacity to carry a person (Zech. 5:6–7). The term is also a unit of measure equivalent to such a vessel.

ephod   An outer garment worn over the shoulders of an official—typically a priest—during religious ceremonies.

Ephraemi   See CODEX EPHRAEMI.

Epic of Gilgamesh   An ancient Babylonian text containing a flood narrative that is strikingly similar to that recorded in Genesis. In this epic, a pious man is commanded in a dream to build a boat that will sustain his family and animals through a catastrophic flood. The only survivors of the flood are those in the boat, which comes to rest on a mountain after birds are sent out in search of habitable land.

epiphany   A physical manifestation of God (Gk., *epiphaneia*, "manifestation"), such as the burning bush (Ex. 3), the pillars of cloud and fire that accompanied the Israelites during the EXODUS (Ex. 13:21–22), and the cloud that filled SOLOMON'S TEMPLE at its dedication (1 Kings 8:10–13).

epistemology   The branch of philosophy dealing with the nature of knowledge and its origin (Gk., *episteme*, "knowledge").

epistle   A letter in the New Testament (i.e., Romans–Jude; from Gk. *epistole*). Also known as epistolary literature.

E

eros   Greek for sexual love.

eschatology   The branch of THEOLOGY concerned with the study of last things (Gk., *eschatos*, "last thing"), including the SEC-OND COMING of Christ, the judgment, the RESURRECTION of the dead, HELL, and eternal life. See also MILLENNIUM and TRIBULA-TIONAL VIEWS.

eschaton   The end times (Gk., *eschatos*, "last thing"). See also ESCHATOLOGY.

Essenes   A first-century Jewish sect in PALESTINE characterized by initiation rites, regimented codes of conduct, and eschatological enthusiasm awaiting the arrival of two Messiahs. Many identify the Essenes as the inhabitants of the QUMRAN complex on the northwestern shore of the Dead Sea and collectors of the DEAD SEA SCROLLS.

essentialism   A belief system that defines human life corporately by considering the fundamental nature of humankind rather than individually through human experience (i.e., EXISTENTIALISM).

eternal life   Life that never ends. For believers, eternal life is both a present reality (John 3:36) and a future possession (Luke 18:30). The term is one of quality (John 17:3) as well as duration (John 6:51).

eternal security   The doctrine that one's SALVATION is irrevocable and incapable of being lost (see John 5:24; 6:39–40; 10:27–29; Rom. 8:38–39; 1 Cor. 3:12–15; Eph. 1:13–14). Those who claim that salvation can be lost seek support in passages such as Ezekiel 18:24; Matthew 12:31; Romans 11:21–22; 1 Corinthians 6:9–10; 2 Timothy 2:12; Hebrews 6:4–6; and Revelation 3:16. See also ASSURANCE OF SALVATION.

eternal sonship   The belief that Jesus' sonship did not have a beginning. This view contrasts with ADOPTIONISM and others that claim that Jesus became the Son of God at his BAPTISM or possibly at his INCARNATION.

ethos   The personality, credibility, or individual character of a speaker or writer, or of a group or institution, or of a text itself.

etiology   The explanation of the origin of a custom, tradition, name, or practice, usually through a MYTH or FABLE (Gk., *aitia*, "cause"). For example, the sin in the Garden of Eden explains why humans fear serpents and why women experience pain during labor (Gen. 3).

etymology   The history and evolution of a word, including changes in a word's meaning and form as it was transmitted over time and possibly from one language to another.

Eucharist   COMMUNION; the Lord's Supper. The name probably derives from the prayer of thanks offered by Jesus before partaking of the bread and wine in the Upper Room (Gk., *eucharisteo*, "to give thanks").

eunuch   A palace official in the courts of ancient Near Eastern kingdoms who was likely responsible for the king's HAREM and who was sometimes castrated to ensure the protection of the king's wives. The term can also refer to any castrated male (Matt. 19:12).

euphemism   A polite way of saying something judged to be offensive or vulgar. Scribes occasionally provided euphemisms in the margins of biblical manuscripts where the wording of the text seemed too strong (e.g., "lain with" in the American Standard Version in place of "ravished" in Jer. 3:2).

Eutychianism   See MONOPHYSITISM.

evangelical In American Protestantism, a designation for one who places particular emphasis on the authority of the Bible, the GOSPEL, evangelism, and the need for personal conversion (Gk., *euangelion*, "good news").

evangelist In New Testament studies, one of the Gospel writers (Gk., *euangelistes*, "one who brings good news"); or more broadly of one entrusted with the gospel message (Acts 21:8; Eph. 4:11; 2 Tim. 4:5).

evening sacrifice The second of two daily offerings prescribed in the MOSAIC LAW in which flawless, one-year-old lambs were sacrificed (Ex. 29:38–41; Num. 28:3–8).

E

evidentialism A branch of APOLOGETICS that argues for the existence of God and credibility of Christianity by presenting evidence and scientific proofs with the assumption that evangelism in large part involves persuasion of unbelievers through the force of logical argumentation.

evolution The theory that human and animal life originated by a natural process of morphological and physiological adaptations from simple to more complex forms over millions of years. THEISTIC EVOLUTION claims that an intelligent being superintended this process. See also CREATIONISM.

ex cathedra Latin, "from the chair" (i.e., authoritatively). Used to describe the infallible speech of the pope when communicating officially on matters of faith and practice. See also INFALLIBILITY, PAPAL.

ex nihilo Latin, "out of nothing." Used to describe the biblical account of creation in which no preexisting materials were used.

excommunication The official removal of a rebellious church member from the fellowship of believers, as prescribed by Jesus in Matthew 18:15–17 (see also 1 Cor. 5).

exegesis Interpretation of a text (Gk., *exegesis*, "to lead out"). Biblical exegesis involves the study of words, SYNTAX, grammar, THEOLOGY, and so on, to uncover the meaning of a passage.

exemplarism A view of the ATONEMENT that stresses Jesus' moral example in dying on the cross. Thus believers are moved to repentance and obedience as they contemplate God's love and the self-sacrifice of Christ.

Exile, the See BABYLONIAN CAPTIVITY.

E

existentialism A belief system that defines human life individually through human experience rather than corporately by considering the fundamental nature of humankind (i.e., ESSENTIALISM). It is formally traced to the writings of Søren Kierkegaard (1813–1855) and Friedrich Nietzsche (1844–1900).

Exodus, the The liberation of the Israelites from Egyptian enslavement (Gk., *ex hodos*, "a path out"). Following the ten plagues, Pharaoh released the Israelites, and they were led out by Moses through the Red Sea (Ex. 12:31–42; 14:1–31).

exorcism The casting out of an evil spirit. Exorcisms were performed by Jesus (Mark 1:25–26; 9:38–39) and the apostles (Mark 6:7; Acts 16:18).

expiation ATONEMENT for sins by SACRIFICE, which removes the barrier of SIN between God and people. The Old Testament prescribes expiatory sacrifices for sin; in the New Testament, expiation is accomplished through the death of Christ (Rom. 3:25; 1 John 2:2; 4:10). Expiation is somewhat synonymous with

PROPITIATION, though the former emphasizes the removal of sin whereas the latter emphasizes the turning aside of God's wrath.

Expulsion, the   Traditional name for God's banishment of Adam and Eve from the Garden of Eden (Gen. 3:23–24).

external evidence   In TEXTUAL CRITICISM, the evidence for a particular manuscript READING pertaining to the date and character (i.e., reliability) of the manuscripts themselves. This is in contrast to INTERNAL EVIDENCE, which weighs the habits and tendencies of SCRIBES, as well as matters related to the biblical passage itself (INTRINSIC PROBABILITY).

E

extrabiblical   An adjective designating anything outside the Bible. Extrabiblical literature that dates from the time of the Bible is studied for background information. For example, the Apocrypha shed light on the INTERTESTAMENTAL PERIOD.

extracanonical   See NONCANONICAL.

extreme unction   One of seven sacraments in the Roman Catholic Church in which a priest or BISHOP prays over an individual who is on the brink of death. The recipient of this rite is sometimes anointed with oil (James 5:14–15).

F

fable A fictitious story, sometimes involving animals and inanimate objects that speak (Judg. 9:7–15; 2 Kings 14:9).

faith Trust or belief, even in the absence of conclusive evidence (Heb. 11:1). Apparently even the smallest quantity of faith is surprisingly powerful (Luke 17:6). The disciples were repeatedly rebuked by Jesus for their lack of faith (Matt. 6:30; 8:26; 14:31; 16:8; Mark 4:40; 6:6; Luke 8:25). Faith is the prerequisite for forgiveness (Acts 10:43; James 5:15), and often Jesus is the stated object of faith (John 2:11; 7:31; 8:30; 11:45; 12:11; Acts 3:16). In later New Testament books (e.g., the PASTORAL EPISTLES), "the faith" denotes a body of accepted Christian beliefs.

Fall, the The sin of Adam and Eve in the Garden of Eden and its consequences (Gen. 3). Paul writes that SIN, guilt, and death entered the world through this act of disobedience, thereby affecting all humankind (Rom. 5:12).

fallen angels Immaterial beings whose SIN led to their removal from HEAVEN and subsequent imprisonment (2 Peter 2:4; Jude 6). Many believe that DEMONS are fallen angels who have been permitted to be involved in human affairs (Job 1:7; 2:2).

false prophet, the The eschatological figure who performs miraculous signs and deceives humanity, causing them to worship the first beast of Revelation (Rev. 13:11–18). The false prophet comes out of the earth, is identified as the second beast, and is cast into the lake of fire along with the first beast (Rev. 19:20; see also Matt. 24:24; Rev. 16:13).

far demonstrative In grammar, a pronoun that refers to something relatively far away from the speaker or writer, as with "that" and "those." The opposite of NEAR DEMONSTRATIVE.

fasting Abstaining from food and water or, in some instances, from food only. The Old Testament stipulates a fast on the Day of Atonement (Lev. 23:27, 29, 32; see also Acts 27:9). Jesus fasted during his temptation (Matt. 4:2; Luke 4:2) and warns elsewhere against fasting to impress people (Matt. 6:16–18).

F

fatalism The belief that all of human existence is predetermined and cannot be changed. Fatalism is thought to lead to despair or licentiousness among its adherents. See also DETERMINISM.

fathers See PATRISTIC ERA.

Feast of Booths See FEAST OF TABERNACLES.

Feast of Dedication See FEAST OF LIGHTS.

Feast of Firstfruits See FEAST OF WEEKS.

Feast of Harvest See FEAST OF WEEKS.

Feast of Ingathering See FEAST OF TABERNACLES.

Feast of Lights An eight-day Jewish celebration beginning on the twenty-fifth of Kislev (November/December) and commemorating the restoration and consecration of the TEMPLE under the MACCABEES (165/164 B.C.E.). Tradition says that after the dedication of the temple, a seven-branched MENORAH miraculously burned for eight days using only one day's worth of oil. Also known as the Feast of Dedication (John 10:22) or in Hebrew, Hanukkah. See also MACCABEAN REVOLT.

Feast of New Moon   See FEAST OF TRUMPETS.

Feast of Passover   Annual commemoration of the "passing over" of the angel of death prior to the tenth plague and the Israelites' EXODUS from Egypt (Ex. 12–13). The festival began on the fourteenth of Nisan (April/May) and together with the FEAST OF UNLEAVENED BREAD, which immediately followed, lasted eight days.

Feast of Pentecost   See FEAST OF WEEKS.

Feast of Purim   An annual two-day festival held on the fourteenth and fifteenth of Adar (February/March) and commemorating the deliverance of the Jews from Haman's efforts to annihilate them (Est. 9:19–32). "Purim" is an Akkadian loanword for "lots," referring to the lots cast by Haman to determine the day to begin Jewish extermination (Est. 3:7; 9:24).

Feast of Tabernacles   An annual commemoration of God's provision for Israel during her wanderings in the wilderness following the EXODUS (Lev. 23:33–43; Num. 29:12–40). This feast begins five days after the DAY OF ATONEMENT, on the fifteenth of Tishri (September/October), and requires participants to live for seven days in shelters made from branches. The Feast of Tabernacles was one of three major feasts in Israel (called "pilgrim feasts"), including also the FEAST OF WEEKS and the FEAST OF UNLEAVENED BREAD (Deut. 16:16). Also known as the Feast of Booths or the Feast of Ingathering.

Feast of Trumpets   An annual celebration held on the first day of Tishri (September/October) that involved special sacrifices and trumpet blasts (Lev. 23:23–25; Num. 29:1). Following the Babylonian exile, the Feast of Trumpets also commemorated the Jewish New Year (ROSH HASHANAH). Also known as Feast of New Moon.

Feast of Unleavened Bread   An annual, seven-day feast from the fifteenth to the twenty-first of Abib (April/May), during which no work is done and no yeast is consumed in order to commemorate the haste with which the Israelites left Egypt during the EXODUS (Ex. 12:1–20; 23:15; Deut. 16:1–8). The Feast of Unleavened Bread, which begins the day following the FEAST OF PASSOVER and is often associated with it, was one of three major feasts in Israel (called "pilgrim feasts"), including also the FEAST OF WEEKS and the FEAST OF TABERNACLES (Deut. 16:16).

Feast of Weeks   An annual Jewish celebration observed at the beginning of wheat harvest in early summer (Deut. 16:9–12). Since it occurred seven weeks or fifty days after the FEAST OF PASSOVER, it also became known as PENTECOST (meaning "fiftieth day"). The Feast of Weeks was one of three major feasts in Israel (called "pilgrim feasts"), including also the FEAST OF UNLEAVENED BREAD and the FEAST OF TABERNACLES (Deut. 16:16). Also known as the Feast of Firstfruits and Feast of Harvest.

federal headship   A view of ORIGINAL SIN that states that Adam was not acting merely on his own behalf during the FALL but served as representative of the entire human race. Thus, the guilt and consequences of the Fall, including SIN and death, extend rightfully to all humanity (see Gen. 3; Rom. 5:12, 17–19). See also NATURAL HEADSHIP.

fellowship   Companionship, whether among believers (Acts 2:42) or between a believer and God (1 John 1:3–7).

fellowship offering   See PEACE OFFERING.

88

feminine   In Greek, Hebrew, and Aramaic, nouns and other words are either masculine, feminine, or (in Greek only) neuter. Other words will agree in gender with those that they modify.

feminist theology   A twentieth-century movement mainly in the United States, which sought to raise awareness of the distinct identity and experiences of women. Some have considered feminist theology a subcategory of LIBERATION THEOLOGY, since release from oppression is a central theme.

Fertile Crescent   The crescent-shaped area of land extending from the Persian Gulf in the east to the Mediterranean Sea in the West, including ancient MESOPOTAMIA, SYRIA, and PALESTINE. The Fertile Crescent receives its irrigation primarily from the Tigris and Euphrates Rivers and was the cradle of many ancient Near Eastern civilizations.

fertility god/goddess   A DEITY associated with agricultural success and human reproduction. According to the view of some cultures in the ancient Near East, the success of one's crops and the ability to procreate was dependent on appeasing the fertility god(s)/goddess(es). BAAL, a Canaanite deity represented by a bull, was a symbol of male fertility and thought to be the "god of the storm," bringing rain for crops.

festival scrolls   See MEGILLOTH.

fiat creationism   The view that God created the universe and everything in it directly and virtually instantaneously (Lat., *fiat*, "let it be done"). This contrasts with THEISTIC EVOLUTION or PROGRESSIVE CREATIONISM, both of which view creation as a gradual process.

fideism   A theological system that downplays reason and emphasizes faith as a means of acquiring truth (Lat., *fides*, "faith").

According to fideism, truth is embraced strictly on faith because of the ostensible insufficiency of the human mind.

figurative   Of or related to language that cannot be construed literally because of symbolism, HYPERBOLE, or other literary techniques. The Bible frequently employs figurative language (see Amos 4:1; Matt. 18:9; John 16:25; Gal. 4:24). See also ALLEGORY.

filioque **controversy**   The disagreement between the medieval Eastern and Western churches over the inclusion of the term "*filioque*" (Lat., "and [from] the Son") in the Nicene Creed as a description of the provider of the Holy Spirit. The Eastern church maintained that the Holy Spirit proceeded only from the Father (John 15:26). By the ninth century, however, nearly all Western churches had added the word to their version of the CREED, in part to combat ARIANISM. Many think that the East-West church schism of 1054 C.E. had roots in the *filioque* controversy.

finitism   In theology, the belief that God's power is limited (Lat., *finire*, "to limit"). See also OMNIPOTENCE.

First Advent   See ADVENT.

first cause   The eternal, unchanging, and intelligent "cause" (i.e., God) responsible for the "effect," which is the universe. God as the First Cause is often mentioned in connection with the COSMOLOGICAL ARGUMENT for the existence of God.

first deportation   The initial banishment from Jerusalem in 606/605 B.C.E., when the nobility of JUDAH—including Daniel—were led captive to Babylonia (2 Chron. 36:6–7; Dan. 1:1–4). The BABYLONIAN CAPTIVITY was accomplished in three consecutive deportations, culminating in the 587/586 B.C.E. destruction of Jerusalem.

first person of the Trinity   Designation for God the Father. See also TRINITY.

First Temple period   The interval from the erection of SOLOMON'S TEMPLE in the tenth century B.C.E. (1 Kings 6; 2 Chron. 3) until its destruction by the Babylonians in 586 B.C.E. (2 Kings 25:9; 2 Chron. 36:19).

firstborn   The first offspring. In the Old Testament God demanded that firstborn male animals be sacrificed to him (Ex. 13:12). Firstborn male children were afforded a BIRTHRIGHT and a double portion of the family's inheritance (Deut. 21:15–17); they were especially cherished, making the final plague against the Egyptians—the death of the firstborn (Ex. 12:1–30)—particularly severe. In the New Testament, Jesus is Mary's firstborn (Luke 2:7) as well as the "firstborn from [among] the dead" (Col. 1:18; Rev. 1:5).

F

firstfruits   The initial harvest of the season. According to MOSAIC LAW, the agricultural firstfruits were to be given to God in the form of offerings and sacrifices (Ex. 23:16, 19; Lev. 23:10, 17). Believers are sometimes called God's firstfruits (Jer. 2:3; James 1:18), and Jesus is referred to as the "firstfruits" from the dead (1 Cor. 15:20, 23).

five-case system   In GREEK, a method of classifying words that have CASE into five cases (i.e., NOMINATIVE, GENITIVE, DATIVE, ACCUSATIVE, and VOCATIVE), based on their form. This is in contrast to the EIGHT-CASE SYSTEM, which classifies words based on their function in context.

Five Scrolls   See MEGILLOTH.

flesh   In theology, the seat of lust and sinful passions (Rom. 7:18; 1 Cor. 3:1–3; Gal. 5:16–21) or the hopeless efforts of humankind to attain SALVATION by works (Gal. 3:3; Phil. 3:3). Flesh can also denote the material component of humankind as opposed to the immaterial SPIRIT or SOUL. See also CARNAL.

flight to Egypt   Joseph and his family's journey from Bethlehem to Egypt to escape Herod's search for the child Jesus (Matt. 2:13–15).

Flood, the   See GENESIS FLOOD.

footwashing   Washing someone's feet as an expression of service, following Jesus' example recorded in John 13:2–11. Some Christians, heeding Jesus' command to wash one another's feet (13:14–15; "do as I have done for you"), view footwashing as a SACRAMENT, in addition to COMMUNION and BAPTISM.

F

forbearance   Patient endurance under provocation. For example, God exercises forbearance when dealing with sinners (Rom. 3:25).

forbidden fruit   The fruit from the tree of the knowledge of good and evil in the Garden of Eden that God commanded Adam not to eat (Gen. 2:16–17).

forefather   A male ancestor. In the Bible, forefathers may denote blood ancestors (Ex. 13:5) or spiritual ancestors (2 Tim. 1:3) or, for a Jew, whole generations of Israelites (Neh. 9:9; John 6:31).

foreknowledge   Knowing something before it occurs (Acts 2:23). In THEOLOGY, God's pretemporal knowledge of those he would save (Rom. 8:29). Sometimes used interchangeably with PREDESTINATION and ELECTION.

forensic justification   The doctrine that human beings are declared—not made—righteous by God in SALVATION (Rom. 4:3,

5, 9, 22). Thus, forensic justification views God as a judge who acquits a guilty party (Ps. 9:4). Also called forensic righteousness.

foreordination   See PREDESTINATION.

foreshadowing   In literary studies, the technique of giving the reader a glimpse or suggestion of an upcoming person or event. For example, Manasseh, the wicked king of Judah, foreshadows Israel's exile and restoration as he is taken into captivity in Babylon and then allowed to return to Jerusalem following his repentance (2 Chron. 33:11–13). See also TYPOLOGICAL INTERPRETATION.

forgiveness   Absolution of sin or offense, extended by God (Isa. 43:25; Mark 2:7) or some person (Matt. 18:35; Col. 3:13). In the Old Testament, forgiveness involves ATONEMENT (usually by sacrifice), enabling believers to have a relationship with God. In the New Testament, forgiveness of sins comes only through Jesus Christ (Matt. 26:28; Luke 24:47). Blasphemy of the Holy Spirit is designated the UNFORGIVABLE SIN (Matt. 12:31–32; Mark 3:29; Luke 12:10).

form criticism   The scholarly discipline concerned with reconstructing and analyzing the oral and written traditions that evidently stand behind much of the biblical text. The PENTATEUCH and SYNOPTIC GOSPELS have received much attention in form critical studies. Sometimes called TRADITION CRITICISM. The German term for this discipline is *Formgeschichte*.

formal equivalence   A TRANSLATION method that strives for a literal rendering of the original text, along with attention to the order of words and clauses. See also DYNAMIC EQUIVALENCE.

formal parallelism   In Hebrew poetry, a literary device in which the second line completes the first line. For example, "The city of the Great King" merely completes "MOUNT ZION" of the preceding line in Psalm 48:2.

Former Prophets   The Old Testament books of Joshua, Judges, 1–2 Samuel, and 1–2 Kings (see also DEUTERONOMIC HISTORY). The Former Prophets, together with the LATTER PROPHETS, constitute the second division of the Hebrew Bible, designated "THE PROPHETS."

Formgeschichte   German for "form history." See FORM CRITICISM.

fornication   Sexual immorality (see Matt. 15:19; Gal. 5:19).

Four Document Hypothesis   See L, M, and Q.

four horsemen of the Apocalypse   The four riders on horseback, accompanying the first four seals, who carry out judgment presumably during the TRIBULATION (Rev. 6:1–8; see also Zech. 1:8–17; 6:1–8). The horses' different colors may represent the character of their riders.

frankincense   A resin used in the ancient Near East for medicinal and aromatic purposes (Ex. 30:34–36; Rev. 18:13), and one of the three gifts presented to the child Jesus by the MAGI (Matt. 2:11). Also called incense.

free will   The notion that people are capable of choosing that which they desire, with no intrusion by the will of others (especially God). In the study of SALVATION, the idea that God has relinquished the choice for salvation to each individual. See also DETERMINISM.

Freerianus   See CODEX WASHINGTONENSIS.

freewill offering   A voluntary PEACE OFFERING presented for the purpose of praise or thanksgiving, whose meat was to be consumed within two days (Lev. 7:16–17; 22:18–23).

free-will theism   See OPEN THEISM.

frontlet   See PHYLACTERY.

fruit of the Spirit   The visible evidence of the Holy Spirit in the lives of believers, listed in Galatians 5:22–23 as love, joy, peace, patience, kindness, goodness, faithfulness, gentleness, and self-control.

fullness of time(s)   A New Testament figure of speech referring to the time ordained by God for the coming of Jesus and his accomplishments (Gal. 4:4; Eph. 1:10; cf. Mark 1:15).

F

functional equivalence   See DYNAMIC EQUIVALENCE.

fundamentalism   A transdenominational movement within twentieth-century American Protestantism that emphasizes the INERRANCY of the Bible, the virgin birth, the DEITY of Christ, the substitutionary ATONEMENT, and the future return of Christ. Fundamentalism arose as a reaction to nineteenth-century liberalism and biblical criticism.

future tense   In Greek, the TENSE that ordinarily indicates verbal action in the future.

futuristic view   A view of the book of Revelation that asserts that Revelation 4–22 describes events related to the end times, particularly events associated with the second coming of Christ. See also HISTORICIST VIEW and PRETERIST VIEW.

G

gap theory   A view of creation that says although God created a perfect world, it lost this perfection during an immeasurable time "gap" between Genesis 1:1 and 1:2. Genesis 1:2 should be translated, "Now the earth *became* void and formless," rendering the six days of creation a re-creation. Gap theory adherents are thus able to reconcile the apparent old age of the earth with the biblical record. Also called the restitution theory and ruin-reconstruction theory.

Garden of Gethsemane   The place where Christ was arrested, after he had prayed about his impending death (Matt. 26:36–56; Mark 14:32–51).

Garden of Eden   The paradisiacal garden planted by God in which he placed Adam and Eve (Gen. 2:8–14). In this garden were located the TREE OF LIFE and the TREE OF THE KNOWLEDGE OF GOOD AND EVIL.

Gattung   The German equivalent of the French *genre*. See GENRE.

Gehenna   A valley to the south and west of Jerusalem that forms a natural border between Benjamin and Judah (Heb., "Valley of Hinnom"). Some Israelite kings offered human sacrifices here (2 Chron. 28:3; 33:6), leading Josiah to pronounce the valley defiled (2 Kings 23:10). In the New Testament, Jesus describes

Gehenna (translated "hell") metaphorically as an undesirable place characterized by fire and destruction that is prepared for sinners (Matt. 5:22, 29; Mark 9:47–48). See also HADES, HELL.

Gemara Rabbinic commentary on the MISHNAH, which was eventually incorporated into the TALMUD.

gematria Jewish numerology, in which individuals are identified using Hebrew and/or Greek numbers (number values in Hebrew and Greek were represented by letters). For example, various historical figures have been falsely identified as the beast of Revelation 13:18 because the letters of their names happened to add up to the number "666."

gender In Greek, Hebrew, and Aramaic, nouns and other words are either masculine, feminine, or (in Greek only) neuter. Other words will agree in gender with those they modify.

gender-inclusive text In biblical studies, a TRANSLATION that renders masculine Hebrew and Greek words into gender-neutral English, such as substituting "humankind" for "men" or "man," where appropriate. Some groups advocate that masculine pronouns referring to God be translated using gender-neutral language as well.

genealogy A record of ancestry (Gk., *genea*, "family"). Genealogies in the Bible, which are known to skip generations for the purpose of brevity, provide documentation that traces individuals to a particular ancestor, office, ethnicity, geography, or inheritance (Gen. 5; 1 Chron. 1–9; Ezra 7:1–5; Matt. 1:1–16).

General Epistles See CATHOLIC EPISTLES.

general revelation That which God has made known about his nature and existence to all of humankind through creation (Ps.

19:1–2; Matt. 5:45; Rom. 1:18–20), as opposed to SPECIAL REV-ELATION, the Bible.

generation A period of time or a group of contemporaneous people. In the Bible this flexible term denotes time periods vary-ing from about forty years (e.g., Deut. 2:14) to one hundred years or more (e.g., Gen. 15:13–16). It can also refer to a group of people, often with reference to their character (Gen. 7:1; Matt. 12:45; Luke 11:29).

generationism See TRADUCIANISM.

generic Pertaining to a group or class. In grammar, the term is used of nouns—occasionally even singular nouns—that refer to a group or class. For example, the generic article in Titus 1:7 (lit., "*the* overseer") does not refer to a specific person but to the cate-gory of overseer. Similarly, some terms are generic in their reference to gender even though the term itself may be masculine (e.g., "mankind" in Gen. 6:7). Many today are changing these to more neutral words (e.g., "humankind" or "humanity").

Genesis Flood The catastrophic deluge recorded in Genesis 6–8 through which only Noah's family and the animals on the ARK survived. See also UNIVERSAL FLOOD THEORY and LOCAL FLOOD THEORY.

genitive The grammatical case in GREEK that commonly expresses possession or source (Lat., *gignere*, "to beget").

genitive absolute A construction in Greek entailing a clause that is usually grammatically unrelated to the rest of the sentence (thus "absolute"), which contains a participle in the genitive case and, often, a genitive noun or pronoun. Genitive absolutes usually carry temporal significance, as is the case in Acts 13:2: "While they were worshiping the Lord and fasting...."

genizah   A storage compartment for manuscripts that are no longer used.

genre   A category of literature (Lat., *genus*, "kind") containing characteristic form, subject matter, or style of writing. The Bible contains dozens of literary genres, including PARABLE, NARRATIVE, PROPHECY, FABLE, and poetry.

Gentile   A non-Jew. Sometimes a pejorative designation, similar to the modern "pagan" (Isa. 42:6; Acts 10:45).

Gentile court   An open area in HEROD'S TEMPLE where Gentiles were permitted to gather. Paul was falsely accused of escorting Trophimus the Ephesian beyond the Gentile court into an area restricted for Jews, thus defiling the temple (Acts 21:27–28).

Gethsemane   See GARDEN OF GETHSEMANE.

Gilgamesh Epic   See EPIC OF GILGAMESH.

global flood   See UNIVERSAL FLOOD THEORY and GENESIS FLOOD.

gloria in excelsis   Latin for "glory in the highest" (see Luke 2:14).

glorification   In THEOLOGY, the final stage in the process of SALVATION when God will cleanse believers from all SIN, thereby rendering them spiritually perfect (Rom. 8:23, 30). Glorification occurs instantaneously upon the believer's entrance into HEAVEN, although the glorification of the physical body awaits the RESURRECTION (1 Thess. 4:16). The term can also refer to the eschatological renewal of creation (Rom. 8:20–21).

glory   Majesty, honor, greatness, or fame, usually ascribed to God (Ps. 29:1) or Jesus (John 17:1). Believers look forward to

G

beholding this glory (Matt. 24:30; Rom. 8:18) and even sharing in it (Ps. 73:24; 1 Peter 5:1, 4).

gloss A brief scribal explanation in the margin or between the lines of a MANUSCRIPT.

glossolalia The spiritual gift of SPEAKING IN TONGUES (Gk., *glossa*, "tongue," *lalia*, "speech").

Gnosticism A movement traced to the second century C.E. that emphasized knowledge and enlightenment, the inherent evil of matter, and the goodness of the SPIRIT or SOUL (Gk., *gnosis*, "knowledge"). Gnosticism seemed similar to Christianity, and Gnostics sometimes quoted from the New Testament in defense of their beliefs (such as from 2 Peter 1, which places special emphasis on knowledge).

goad A long staff with at least one pointed end that was used to steer oxen and other animals. Shamgar killed 600 Philistines with a goad (Judg. 3:31). Also called an oxgoad.

God-breathed See INSPIRATION and *THEOPNEUSTOS*.

God-fearer A designation in the book of Acts for a GENTILE who was sympathetic to JUDAISM but had not undergone CIRCUMCISION (Acts 13:26; 17:4, 17).

Godhead A theological designation for the essence of God; likewise God himself (the Godhead), with special reference to the nature of God as TRINITY. The term is often used in discussion of the individual traits of the persons of the Trinity.

goel See KINSMAN-REDEEMER. Also *GO'EL*.

golden calf The IDOL that served as a tangible object of worship for Aaron and the Israelites when Moses failed to return as expected from Mount Sinai (Ex. 32).

Golden Rule A popular title designating Jesus' commandment to "do to others what you would have them to do you" (Matt. 7:12; Luke 6:31). The teaching of the LAW and the Prophets is, according to Jesus, summed up in the Golden Rule.

Golgotha An Aramaic word meaning "skull" and referring to the hill on which Christ was crucified (Matt. 27:33; Mark 15:22; John 19:17). See also CALVARY.

Good Friday The Friday preceding Easter Sunday that commemorates Jesus' CRUCIFIXION.

gopher wood Perhaps an older designation for cypress wood. The material from which Noah's ARK was built (Gen. 6:14).

G

gospel The message about JESUS CHRIST, especially his perfect life, his death on a cross for the sins of the world, and his RESURRECTION from the dead on the third day (1 Cor. 15:1–4). Also designates the ancient books recording these events, whether in the New Testament (i.e., Matthew, Mark, Luke, and John) or APOCRYPHAL (e.g., *Gospel of Bartholomew* and *Infancy Gospel of Thomas*). Translated from the Greek *euangelion*, meaning "good news."

goy/goyim See GENTILE.

grace In theology, the quality of God that enables sinful humankind to experience SALVATION (Acts 15:11; Eph. 2:5, 8). Grace involves forgiveness (Rom. 5:20) and often denotes God's sustaining enablement of believers (Rom. 5:2; 2 Cor. 1:2; Gal. 6:18). The Gospel of John contrasts grace with the MOSAIC LAW (John 1:17).

Graf-Wellhausen theory See DOCUMENTARY HYPOTHESIS.

grain offering A voluntary SACRIFICE during which part of the grain was burnt in worship and the remainder was eaten by the priests (Lev. 2:1–16). The grain offering generally accompanied either the burnt or PEACE OFFERING. One of the five main offerings in Israel (along with the BURNT OFFERING, peace offering, SIN OFFERING, and GUILT OFFERING).

Great Cappadocians   See CAPPADOCIAN FATHERS.

great commandment   Jesus' instruction to "Love the Lord your God with all your heart and with all your SOUL and with all your mind and with all your strength" (Mark 12:30; see also Deut. 6:4–5; Matt. 22:37).

Great Commission   Jesus' command to his disciples to go into all the world, preach the GOSPEL, and make disciples (Matt. 28:19–20).

Great River   The Hebrew name for the Euphrates River.

Great Sea   The Hebrew name for the Mediterranean Sea.

Great Synagogue, the   Body of Jewish leaders and scribes that ostensibly existed after the BABYLONIAN CAPTIVITY, reorganizing religious life of the Jews after the temple was destroyed.

Great Tribulation   The climactic, eschatological outpouring of God's wrath, thought by many to last for seven years. Some reserve this title for the second half of the seven-year TRIBULATION, supposedly when the outpouring of wrath will intensify (Matt. 24:21; Rev. 2:22; 7:14).

Great White Throne   God's throne of judgment, from which all unbelievers will receive their final condemnation into the lake of fire (Rev. 20:11–15). See also GREAT WHITE THRONE JUDGMENT.

Great White Throne judgment God's final judgment of all unbelievers, when the wicked from every age will appear to receive their official condemnation into the lake of fire (Rev. 20:11–15). See also BEMA SEAT.

Greek The language of the NEW TESTAMENT. Also refers to a citizen of Greece or, less commonly, as a synonym for "Gentile" (Gal. 3:28). See also KOINE GREEK.

Greek Old Testament See SEPTUAGINT.

Griesbach hypothesis J. J. Griesbach's (1745–1812) solution to the SYNOPTIC PROBLEM, which proposes that Matthew was the first Gospel written (i.e., MATTHEAN PRIORITY/HYPOTHESIS) among the SYNOPTIC GOSPELS (Matthew, Mark, and Luke); then Luke relied on Matthew; then Mark relied on both Matthew and Luke. Most scholars today hold that Mark was written first (MARKAN PRIORITY/HYPOTHESIS).

guilt offering A mandatory offering of a ram or lamb for the ATONEMENT of an unintentional SIN (Lev. 5:14–6:7; 7:1–10; 14:12). One of the five main offerings in Israel (along with BURNT OFFERING, GRAIN OFFERING, PEACE OFFERING, and SIN OFFERING).

guttural A speech sound pronounced using one's throat (Lat., *guttur*, "throat"). For example, the Hebrew letters *aleph, he, het,* and *ayin*.

Habiru According to the Canaanite Amarna letters (written c. 1400 B.C.E.), a diverse ancient people characterized as marauders. Since the date of the Amarna letters roughly corresponds to the alleged date of Joshua's conquest of Canaan, some have theorized that the Hebrews were the Habiru people. Also spelled Hapiru or Apiru.

Hades The New Testament Greek equivalent of the Old Testament "SHEOL," the place of the dead, conveying darkness and separation from God. Sometimes Hades refers to the abode of the deceased wicked (Luke 16:23; Rev. 20:13–14), the keys to which belong to Christ (Rev. 1:18). Hades is often translated "HELL" (Matt. 16:18) in older translations; along with the reprobate, death, and Satan, Hades will ultimately be cast into the lake of fire (Rev. 20:13–14). See also GEHENNA.

Haggadah Interpretation of the nonlegal material of the Hebrew Scriptures (Heb., *nagad*, "to tell"). Haggadah and HALAKAH represent the two major divisions of Jewish Midrashic literature. Also spelled Aggadah.

Haggadic Adjective related to HAGGADAH.

hagiographa Greek term meaning "holy writings," referring to the third division of the Hebrew Bible, the WRITINGS. Equivalent to the Hebrew "KETUBIM." See also TANAKH.

hagiography   Writing about noteworthy Christians or "saints" (from Gk., *hagios*, "holy one, saint," and *graphein*, "to write"), sometimes used pejoratively of an idealized account.

Halakah   Interpretation of the legal material of the Hebrew Scriptures (Heb., *halak*, "to walk"). Halakah and HAGGADAH represent the two major divisions of Jewish midrashic literature. Also spelled Halakkah or Halacha.

Hallel   Psalms 113–118, collectively sung during the feasts of Passover, Pentecost, and Tabernacles (Heb., "praise"). The term is used generally of any psalm featuring praise or thanksgiving. Psalm 136 is often referred to as "the Great Hallel."

hallelujah   Hebrew for "praise YAHWEH" (Ps. 111:1; Rev. 19:1–6).

H

hallow   To treat in a sacred or holy manner; to revere. For example, in the Lord's prayer, God's name is to be hallowed (Luke 11:2).

hamartiology   In THEOLOGY, the study of SIN (Gk., *hamartia*, "sin"), including its origin, extent, and penalty.

hand   In TEXTUAL CRITICISM, a copyist or scribe. "Original hand" denotes the scribe who first copied the MANUSCRIPT; "later hand" refers to a corrector.

Hanukkah   See FEAST OF LIGHTS.

hapax legomenon   A word that occurs only once in a writing or body of literature (Gk., "once said"). For example, *theopneustos* ("God-breathed") appears in the New Testament only at 2 Timothy 3:16.

haplography   In TEXTUAL CRITICISM, the accidental omission from a MANUSCRIPT of a letter, word, phrase, and so on. Haplography is common in passages in which material is repeated (Gk., *haplous*, "single"). The opposite of DITTOGRAPHY.

harem   Place of residence for the wives of a king or, corporately, the wives themselves (Est. 2:3).

harmonization   In TEXTUAL CRITICISM, a scribe's adaptation of a text to resemble more closely a parallel biblical passage.

harmony   A blending of Matthew, Mark, Luke, and John into a single story. The first harmony was Tatian's *DIATESSARON*. Sometimes the word is used synonymously with "SYNOPSIS," a book that prints the SYNOPTIC GOSPELS (and John when relevant) in parallel columns to highlight their similarities and differences.

Hasidean   See HASIDIM.

Hasidim   Hebrew for "pious ones" (1 Macc. 7:12–18), referring to Jews in the second century B.C.E. who retained their traditions in the face of cultural threats (e.g., HELLENISM). Also spelled Chassidim or Hasideans.

Hasmoneans   HIGH PRIESTS who composed a dynastic succession from the MACCABEAN REVOLT in 167 B.C.E. until 37 B.C.E., when Herod the Great began the Herodian succession. The Hasmonean family ruled over a virtually independent Jewish state.

Haustafeln   German designation for the codes of conduct expected in Christian households, such as the commands in Ephesians 5:21–6:9. Singular, *Haustafel*.

head noun   The governing Hebrew noun or noun equivalent in a clause to which other words (e.g., modifiers) are subordinate.

Likewise in Greek, the governing noun in a construction with a genitive.

heaven   The abode of God, innumerable angels, and eventually believers from all time (Deut. 26:15; Matt. 6:9; 18:10). Heaven is also a designation for the sky (Ps. 19:1–6; Acts 14:17). Also referred to as heavens or heavenly realm.

heavenly realm   See HEAVEN.

Hebraic Christian   See JEWISH CHRISTIAN.

Hebraism   A trait of the HEBREW language that comes through in the GREEK of a passage in the New Testament or the SEPTUAGINT, revealing the writer's SEMITIC influence.

Hebrew   A physical descendant of Abraham, Isaac, and Jacob; an Israelite. The term is probably traced to Abraham's ancestor, Eber (see Gen. 10:24–25; 11:14–26). Also the language of the Israelites, in which nearly all of the OLD TESTAMENT was written.

Hebrew Bible   See HEBREW SCRIPTURES.

Hebrew Scriptures   The OLD TESTAMENT, thus named because nearly all of it was originally written in the HEBREW language for Hebrews (i.e., Israelites).

Heilsgeschichte   German term for "SALVATION HISTORY."

hell   The ultimate destination of unbelievers, characterized by unquenchable fire (Mark 9:43), darkness (Matt. 25:30), and "weeping and gnashing of teeth" (Matt. 13:42). Jesus regularly alludes to GEHENNA—the valley near Jerusalem designated for waste—in describing hell (Matt. 5:22; 23:15; Luke 12:5; see also James 3:6).

Hellenism   Greek culture, especially from Alexander the Great until the Romans conquered the Greeks (Gk., *hellen*, "Greek").

Hellenistic period   The historical period from the end of the fourth century to the beginning of the first century B.C.E.; the height of Greece's international influence.

henotheism   Commitment to one god above others in a polytheistic system (Gk., "one God").

hepatoscopy   The practice of forecasting the future or making a decision by examining a liver (Gk., *hepar*, "liver") or other entrails (Ezek. 21:21).

herem   See BAN.

heresy   Teaching that deviates from established doctrine (Gk., *hairesis*, "choice" [i.e., opinion]; see 2 Peter 2:1).

heretic   One whose teaching deviates from established doctrine (Gk., *hairesis*, "choice" [i.e., opinion]). See also HERESY.

hermeneutics   The science that analyses all the facets of biblical interpretation (Gk., *hermeneuo*, "interpret"). See also EXEGESIS.

Herodians   A Jewish political party loyal to Herod Antipas at the time of Christ. They sometimes accompanied the PHARISEES in opposing Jesus (Matt. 22:16; Mark 3:6; 12:13).

Herod's temple   The Jerusalem TEMPLE as it stood from 20 B.C.E. until its destruction in 70 C.E. and whose massive renovation is attributed to Herod the Great (c. 73–4 B.C.E.).

hesed   HEBREW word variously translated "loyal love," "faithfulness," and "lovingkindness." *Hesed* is most commonly associated with God's covenant love for Israel (Ex. 34:7; Deut. 7:9–12), but is also evident in other binding relationships such as family (Ruth 1:8; 2:20) or close friends (1 Sam. 20:14).

heterodoxy   See HERESY.

Hexapla   A six-column text of the Old Testament produced by ORIGEN (c. 185–c. 254 C.E.) and containing Hebrew, Hebrew transliterated into Greek, the SEPTUAGINT, and Greek versions produced by Aquila, SYMMACHUS, and Theodotion.

Hexateuch   The first six books of the Old Testament, Genesis through Joshua.

hieratic   Cursive HIEROGLYPHIC script that accommodated rapid writing (Gk., *hieratikos*, "priestly").

H

hieroglyphic   An ancient Egyptian pictorial form of writing (Gk., *hieros*, "sacred," and *glyphe*, "carving"). Some hieroglyphic texts provide background information for Old Testament studies.

high place   An ALTAR that was usually erected on a hill or a man-made elevation and was part of Canaanite worship. The Canaanite influence on the Israelites is reflected in the numerous high places in Israel (1 Sam. 9:12–25; 1 Kings 13:32–33; 2 Chron. 21:11).

high priest   Person who held the highest religious office in Israel, responsible for entering the HOLY OF HOLIES on the DAY OF ATONEMENT to sprinkle blood on the MERCY SEAT (Lev. 16:11–17). Aaron was the first to hold this office (Ex. 28:1–4); Annas and Caiaphas were high priests during the time of Christ (Luke 3:2). The author of Hebrews deems Jesus the supreme high priest, since he is free from the weaknesses that plagued all other high priests (Heb. 7:26–28).

High Priestly Prayer, the   Jesus' prayer of intercession for his followers as written in John 17, his longest recorded prayer.

higher criticism   Biblical research encompassing all forms of criticism except TEXTUAL CRITICISM. See also LITERARY CRITICISM.

hill country   Fertile Palestinian land west of the Jordan River featuring mountains and rolling hills. Several important Israelite cities were located in the hill country regions of Judah and Ephraim.

Hillelites   A Jewish rabbinical school that followed the more liberal legal interpretations of Rabbi Hillel. The Hillelites flourished following the destruction of the temple in Jerusalem in 70 C.E.

hiphil   A verbal pattern (i.e., conjugation) in HEBREW that usually denotes causation.

hishtaphel   A rare HEBREW verbal pattern.

historical book   A biblical book that narrates historical events and the lives of people, as opposed to prophecy, poetry, and so on. In the OLD TESTAMENT, Joshua through Esther are historical books; in the NEW TESTAMENT, Matthew through Acts.

historical criticism   The investigation of the Bible and other sources to determine the AUTHORSHIP, date, and HISTORICITY of biblical texts. Other forms of biblical criticism are frequently employed in historical criticism.

historical Jesus   The historical person of Jesus of Nazareth, in contrast to a fictitious, secondhand estimation or portrayal thought by some to exist in the Gospels. Thus some scholars contrast the "Jesus of history" with the "Christ of faith," claiming that the true Jesus has been clouded by the mythological "Christ"

H

portrayed by the New Testament writers and, subsequently, the church. See also QUEST OF THE HISTORICAL JESUS.

historical theology The study of doctrinal developments throughout the church's history, either by tracing one doctrine (e.g., CHRISTOLOGY) from a time in the past to the present, or by completely examining the Christian thought of one era and comparing it to others.

historicist view A view of the book of Revelation that asserts that it forecasts events taking place in history from the first century until the second coming of Christ. Thus the vision was future at the time it was written, but much of it has since taken place. See also FUTURISTIC VIEW and PRETERIST VIEW.

historicity The historical accuracy of a book or any portion of it. For example, some scholars have disputed the historicity of the book of Jonah, regarding it entirely as fiction.

hithpael A verbal pattern (i.e. conjugation) in HEBREW that is characterized by an additional "t" sound and the doubling of the second RADICAL or ROOT letter. Hithpael verbs normally denote REFLEXIVE or repeated action.

hithpalpel A rare HEBREW verbal pattern.

hithpolel A rare HEBREW verbal pattern.

holiness Separation, especially from evil or impurity. Holiness describes God (Ps. 99:9), as well as people (Lev. 11:44–45; 19:2; 20:7; 1 Peter 1:16), objects (Lev. 27:30; Ezek. 48:14), and days (e.g., the Sabbath; see Ex. 31:14). That which is holy is considered "clean"; that which is unholy is deemed "unclean" or "common" (Lev. 10:10).

Holiness Code   Leviticus 17–26. This portion of text contains instructions regarding appropriate morality for servants of a holy God, and the phrase "I am the LORD" occurs over forty times in these chapters.

holocaust   In regard to Israel's sacrificial system, a BURNT OFFERING (Gk., "whole burning") in which the entire sacrifice is consumed by fire (see Lev. 1). Also called burnt offering or whole offering.

Holy Communion   See COMMUNION.

Holy of Holies   Designation for the inner room of the TABERNACLE—and later the TEMPLE—in which the ARK of the covenant was kept. Translated in many modern versions as the Holiest Place or the Most Holy Place. The HIGH PRIEST entered this inner sanctuary only once a year to perform sacrificial rites on the DAY OF ATONEMENT (Lev. 16:1–17; see also Ex. 30:10; Heb. 9:7). In the New Testament, believers are invited into the true Holy of Holies (i.e., God's personal presence) on the basis of Christ's sacrifice (Heb. 10:19–22).

H

Holy Place   The large, front room in the TABERNACLE and TEMPLE, separated from the HOLY OF HOLIES by a curtain.

Holy Spirit   The third person of the TRINITY. In the Old Testament the Holy Spirit is present at creation ("the Spirit of God"; Gen. 1:2) and frequently endows people with the ability to prophesy (e.g., 1 Sam. 10:10; 2 Chron. 24:20) or perform great tasks (e.g., Judg. 14:6). In the New Testament the Spirit descends on Jesus after his baptism (Mark 1:10) and is "poured out" on believers at PENTECOST (Acts 2:1–13). Christians are "sealed" with the Holy Spirit (Eph. 1:13), evidenced by "the fruit of the Spirit" (Gal. 5:22–23). The Holy Spirit is referred to by other names, including "Counselor" (John 14:16, 26; 15:26; 16:7), "Spirit of truth"

(John 14:17; 15:26; 16:13), "Spirit of Jesus Christ" (Phil. 1:19; see Gal. 4:6 and 1 Peter 1:11), and "Spirit of grace" (Heb. 10:29).

holy war   Military conflict serving religious and political purposes. In the Old Testament, holy wars were commissioned by God, who was depicted as fighting in behalf of his subjects (Deut. 20). The presence of the ARK of the covenant among the Israelite army indicated that they were fighting a holy war (1 Sam. 4:5–9).

homily   Short message or sermon of exhortation (often written) carrying a moral theme(s).

homoioarchton   In TEXTUAL CRITICISM, a SCRIBAL ERROR attributable to similar beginnings of words in close proximity in a MANUSCRIPT (Gk., "like beginning").

homoiomeson   In TEXTUAL CRITICISM, a SCRIBAL ERROR attributable to the same letters appearing in the middle of words in close proximity in a MANUSCRIPT (Gk., "like center").

homoioteleuton   In TEXTUAL CRITICISM, a SCRIBAL ERROR attributable to similar endings of words in close proximity in a MANUSCRIPT (Gk., "like ending").

homoiousios   A Greek term meaning "similar essence"; it was used by Arius (c. 255–336 C.E.) and his followers of the nature of Jesus Christ as compared to the nature of the Father. This contrasts with the NICENE CREED (325 C.E.), which states that the Son is of the same essence (*homoousion*) as the Father. See also *HOMOOUSIOS*.

homoousios   A Greek term meaning "same essence," which was used in the NICENE CREED (325 C.E.) of the nature of Jesus Christ as compared to the nature of the Father. This contrasts with Arius (c. 255–336 C.E.) and his followers, who thought that the

OF BIBLE AND THEOLOGY WORDS

Son was of a similar essence (*homoiousion*) as the Father. See also
HOMOIOUSIOS.

hophal A PASSIVE verbal pattern (i.e., conjugation) in HEBREW
that normally denotes causation toward the subject of the sentence.
Hophal verbs are the passive counterpart of HIPHIL verbs.

Horeb Another name for Mount Sinai (Heb., "desert").

hortatory Pertaining to exhortation. Such elements are often
introduced by the expression, "Let us" (Ps. 118:24; Heb. 10:22).
A lengthy passage containing many such appeals is referred to as a
hortatory discourse.

hosanna Greek form of the Hebrew word used in Psalm
118:25, meaning "save." It was shouted by the crowds during
Jesus' Triumphal Entry (Matt. 21:9; John 12:13).

house arrest Criminal confinement to a minimum-security
house, which allowed for less restricted visitation (see Acts
28:30–31).

house, household Pertaining to one's living family (1 Sam.
20:14–16) or, in the case of a king, to his dynasty (1 Kings
12:20, 26).

household code See HAUSTAFELN.

household god A figurine that replicates a god and is kept in
one's home.

hydromancy The practice of forecasting the future or con-
sulting spirits or mediums through the use of water (Gk., *hydor*,
"water," and *manteia*, "divination"). Genesis 44:5 may provide an
example.

Hyksos Semitic people whose military skills proved superior to that of the Egyptians during the eighteenth and seventeenth centuries B.C.E.

hymn A song that praises God (Eph. 5:19; Col. 3:16). In biblical studies, the term also designates poetic language (usually in Paul's writings) that may have been drawn from an existing song (e.g., Phil. 2:6–11).

hyperbole A figure of speech in which something is exaggerated, often for emphasis or rhetorical effect (Matt. 19:23–24; Mark 9:42–47).

hyperdispensationalism See ULTRADISPENSATIONALISM.

hypostasis The substance or essence of something. In THEOLOGY, variously denoting the three "persons" of the TRINITY (i.e., Father, Son, and Holy Spirit) or the two "substances" or natures in the person of Christ (i.e., human and divine).

hypostatic union The coexistence of the divine and human in the person of Jesus (Gk., *hypostasis*, "substance"). Thus Jesus is said to be fully God and fully man at the same time without compromise or confusion of the two natures.

hypotaxis The dependent relationship between clauses that contain conjunctions (Gk., "to arrange under"). See also PARATAXIS.

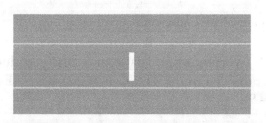

I.N.R.I.   Abbreviation for the Latin, *Iesus Nazarenus Rex Iudae-orum*, "Jesus of Nazareth, king of the Jews" (John 19:19–20). See also *TITULUS*.

ichthys   Greek word meaning "fish." In the early church, *ichthys* served as an acronym in Greek for "Jesus Christ, Son of God, Savior," and its symbol (a rudimentary drawing of a fish) was a sign for Jesus. Also spelled *ichthus*.

iconoclast   A pejorative designation for someone opposed to the use of images in worship (Lat., "destroyer of images").

iconoclastic controversy   The East-West church dispute over the use of images (e.g., of Jesus, Mary, saints) in worship. In general, the Eastern Church advocated the use of images while the Western church opposed it. The iconoclastic controversy reached its climax in the eighth and ninth centuries.

iconodule   A designation for someone sympathetic to the use of images in worship (Gk., "worshiper of images"). Interchangeable with ICONOPHILE.

iconography   Pictorial writing (e.g., Egyptian HIEROGLYPHIC).

iconophile   A pejorative designation for someone sympathetic to the use of images in worship (Gk., "lover of images"). Interchangeable with ICONODULE.

idol   An IMAGE or a false god.

idolatry   Worship of an IMAGE or a false god. Idolatry was expressly forbidden in the TEN COMMANDMENTS (Ex. 20:4–5; Deut. 5:8–9).

illumination   Work of the Holy Spirit that enables someone to recognize the truth of the gospel (see 1 Thess. 1:5; 2:13), discern truth in general (see John 16:13–16), or discover the meaning of a passage (see 2 Peter 1:19).

image   A representation of something or someone. Humankind is made in the image of God (Gen. 1:26–27; James 3:9). The Old Testament forbids the manufacture or worship of any image of a DEITY (Ex. 20:4–6).

imago Dei   A Latin term meaning "image of God," suggesting similarities of human beings to God and the capacity to relate to him (Gen. 1:26–27). Theologians have disagreed as to the precise meaning and implications of the term.

immaculate conception   In Roman Catholic theology, the teaching that Mary, the mother of Jesus, received immunity from ORIGINAL SIN at her conception (Lat., *im*, "without," and *macula*, "stain, blemish").

immaculists   Those who hold that Mary, the mother of Jesus, was free from the taint of ORIGINAL SIN (Lat., *im*, "without," and *macula*, "stain, blemish").

immanence   The obvious presence and activity of God in nature and history, which conveys the nearness of God to his creation (Acts 17:28). This contrasts with God's TRANSCENDENCE, his being above and separate from his creation (Rom. 9:5).

Immanuel Hebrew for "God with us," usually in reference to Jesus (Isa. 7:14; 8:8; Matt. 1:23). Also spelled Emmanuel.

imminence In THEOLOGY, the view that the SECOND COMING of Christ could occur at any time, with no intervening events. See also PRETRIBULATIONISM.

immutability In THEOLOGY, the unchangeableness of God, pertaining especially to his nature, character, and promises (Mal. 3:6; James 1:17). Passages that suggest God's susceptibility to emotions or change (e.g., Gen. 6:6; Hos. 11:8; Jonah 3:10) must be otherwise explained (i.e., ANTHROPOPATHISM).

impassibility In THEOLOGY, the view that God remains completely unaffected by his creation, particularly in regard to suffering or pain. Passages that suggest God's susceptibility to emotions or change (e.g., Gen. 6:6; Hos. 11:8; Jonah 3:10) must be otherwise explained (i.e., ANTHROPOPATHISM). See also PASSIBILITY.

impeccability In THEOLOGY, the inability of Jesus Christ to SIN. This contrasts with PECCABILITY, which states that he could have sinned but did not.

imperfect tense In Hebrew, a verbal INFLECTION that conveys progressive action whether in the past, present, or future. In Greek, the verb TENSE that ordinarily denotes ongoing past action. See also JUSSIVE.

imprecatory psalm A psalm in which a CURSE of misfortune or death is called down on the enemy of the PSALMIST (Pss. 59; 69).

imputation A legal credit or charge to an account. In Protestant THEOLOGY, the SIN and guilt of Adam is imputed to every person (Rom. 5:12–19), while the righteousness of God/Christ is said

119

to be instantaneously imputed, not infused, to the believer upon conversion (Rom. 4:3, 22). See also INFUSION.

incantation   A prayer, spell, or charm steeped in superstition, usually spoken to coerce one's DEITY for protection.

incarnation   The view that the second person of the TRINITY took on a human nature, including flesh (from Lat., *caro*, "flesh"; see John 1:14).

incipient Gnosticism   Gnostic doctrine and ideas that appeared before the second century C.E., when the system was fully developed. See also GNOSTICISM.

inclusio   A literary device in which a word or expression brackets a portion of text by introducing and concluding it (e.g., Eccl. 4:4–16).

I

indulgences   Pardons purchased in order to reduce or cancel one's punishment for SIN. The sale of indulgences by the Catholic Church to reduce time spent in PURGATORY was largely the impetus for the publication of Martin Luther's ninety-five theses on October 31, 1517, traditionally the date the REFORMATION began.

indwell   To reside in someone or something as a permanent presence. In THEOLOGY, the Holy Spirit indwells the believer (John 14:16–17; Eph. 1:13–14), rendering the believer's body the temple of the Holy Spirit (1 Cor. 6:19).

inerrancy   Without error. In THEOLOGY, the doctrine that the Bible, in its original MANUSCRIPTS, was free from error and contradiction. For some, inerrancy pertains to the Bible's teaching on faith and practice alone, while for others the doctrine encompasses the historical, scientific, and "nonreligious" material of the Bible as well. See also INFALLIBILITY.

infallibility   In THEOLOGY, the inability of the Bible to err. For some, infallibility pertains to the Bible's teaching on faith and practice alone, while for others the doctrine encompasses the historical, scientific, and "nonreligious" material of the Bible as well. See also INERRANCY.

infallibility, papal   In CATHOLICISM, the inability of the pope to err when speaking *EX CATHEDRA* ("from the chair," i.e., authoritatively) in matters of faith and practice.

infancy Gospel   An apocryphal account of Jesus' birth and early childhood (e.g., *Infancy Gospel of Thomas*).

infant baptism   The Christian rite of sprinkling babies or young children with water or dipping them completely. The purpose of infant baptism differs according to denomination. The New Testament contains no clear examples of infant baptism, though some assume that young children were present during New Testament baptisms of entire households (Acts 16:15, 33; 18:8; 1 Cor. 1:16). Also called PAEDOBAPTISM. See also BAPTISM.

inflection   Change in a word's form to indicate grammatical functions and relations.

infralapsarianism   In CALVINISM, the position that God's ELECTION of those he planned to save logically followed his decree to permit the FALL (Lat., *infra*, "later," and *lapse*, "fall"). This contrasts with SUPRALAPSARIANISM, which claims that God's election of individuals preceded his decree to permit the Fall (Lat., *supra*, "above," and *lapse*, "fall"). See also SUBLAPSARIANISM.

infusion   The addition of a quality to an existing condition. In Roman Catholic THEOLOGY, the RIGHTEOUSNESS of God is said to be infused gradually into the believer's life, as opposed to being imputed. See also IMPUTATION.

inner man   One's interior true self or heart, as opposed to the visible, exterior body (2 Cor. 4:16).

inspiration   In THEOLOGY, the supernatural process whereby God influenced the biblical writers to record the words of Scripture, thereby rendering it the Word of God (2 Tim. 3:16; 2 Peter 1:21). See also THEOPNEUSTOS.

integral parallelism   See CLIMACTIC PARALLELISM.

intercession   Mediation in behalf of another. The LEVITICAL PRIESTHOOD was established for the purpose of intercession between the sinful nation of Israel and their holy God. In the New Testament, Christ is said to intercede perpetually for the saints (Rom. 8:34; Heb. 7:25; 1 John 2:1), and intercessory prayer is encouraged (1 Tim. 2:1; James 5:14–16).

interlinear Bible   A text containing the Bible (or simply the Old or New Testament) in its original language and a TRANSLATION written in alternating lines.

intermediate state   The interim condition of the Christian between physical death and the future RESURRECTION of the body.

internal evidence   In TEXTUAL CRITICISM, the evidence for a particular manuscript READING pertaining to the habits and tendencies of SCRIBES, as well as matters related to the biblical passage itself (INTRINSIC PROBABILITY), such as the larger context and sense of the passage under scrutiny, the biblical author's vocabulary and style, and so on. This is in contrast to EXTERNAL EVIDENCE, which considers the date and character of the manuscripts themselves.

interpretation   See EXEGESIS.

interrogative prefix   In HEBREW, a letter attached to the beginning of a word, thereby forming a question.

intertestamental period   A term that denotes approximately the two hundred-year period between the last Old Testament book written (and the historical period it describes) and the first New Testament book written (and the historical period it describes). Daniel and some of the books in the APOCRYPHA detail a portion of the history of the intertestamental period, including the MACCABEAN REVOLT and the institution of the FEAST OF HANUKKAH.

intransitive verb   A VERB that does not require a direct object to complete its meaning. For example, "wept" is intransitive in the sentence "Jesus wept" (John 11:35). See also TRANSITIVE VERB.

intrinsic probability   In TEXTUAL CRITICISM, issues pertaining to the likelihood of a textual VARIANT being ORIGINAL based on the biblical passage's wider context, the author's style, vocabulary, and so on. Intrinsic probability and scribal tendencies together provide INTERNAL EVIDENCE in textual criticism, in contrast to EXTERNAL EVIDENCE, which considers the date and character of the manuscripts themselves.

instrumental   Of linguistic forms and constructions that denote means, agency, or cause. In Hebrew and Greek the term is used generally of language features that signify these ideas (e.g., the instrumental prefix "beth" in Hebrew, sometimes meaning "by"). In Greek the term can refer to a separate CASE in the EIGHT-CASE SYSTEM. See also DATIVE.

inverted parallelism   See CHIASM.

invisible church   All Christians everywhere from all time; the UNIVERSAL CHURCH. This contrasts with the visible church, denoting various local assemblies. See also CATHOLIC.

ipsissima verba   Latin for "the very words," referring to certain words recorded in the Gospels that have been deemed by scholars to reflect Jesus' speech verbatim. See also *IPSISSIMA VOX*.

ipsissima vox Latin for "the very voice," referring to certain words attributed to Jesus in the Gospels that bear the marks of summarization or repackaging by the Gospel writer, but that still convey the essence of what was said. See also IPSISSIMA VERBA.

Iron Age I The era from 1200 to 1000 B.C.E. in the ancient Near East.

Iron Age II The era from 1000 to 586 B.C.E. in the ancient Near East.

irresistible grace One of the five points of CALVINISM (the "I" in TULIP), which states that the grace (or invitation) extended by God to the ELECT cannot be resisted. See also EFFECTUAL CALL and CALVINISM, FIVE POINTS OF.

Isaiah Scroll A complete copy of Isaiah found among the DEAD SEA SCROLLS and dating from around 150 B.C.E. The text of this well-preserved twenty-four-foot SCROLL is remarkably similar to copies of Isaiah dating one thousand years later. Also called St. Mark's Isaiah Scroll.

Israel The nation comprised of the physical descendants of Jacob, son of Isaac, son of Abraham (God changed Jacob's name to "Israel" in Gen. 32:28).

issue of blood A menstrual cycle, which according to the Old Testament temporarily rendered a woman CEREMONIALLY UNCLEAN (Lev.15:32–33; see Luke 8:43–44).

ittur sopherim In TEXTUAL CRITICISM, a Hebrew term meaning scribal omission.

J

J According to the DOCUMENTARY HYPOTHESIS, the "Yahwist" source in the PENTATEUCH, supposedly representing the earliest of the literary strata therein (J-E-D-P). The J source customarily refers to God as "Yahweh" ("J" reflects the German spelling "Jahweh").

Jacob's ladder The stairway on which angels of God ascended and descended in Jacob's dream at Bethel (Gen. 28:12). During this dream God stood above the "ladder" and confirmed the ABRAHAMIC COVENANT through Jacob's line (28:13–15).

Jebel Musa The traditional site of Mount Sinai in the southern region of the Sinai Peninsula.

JEDP See DOCUMENTARY HYPOTHESIS.

Jehovah An alternative English pronunciation of the covenant name of God, YAHWEH. In the Middle Ages, scribes customarily wrote the Hebrew vowels from "ADONAI" into the consonants YHWH as a reminder that the divine name should not be pronounced (they would say "Adonai"). From this hybrid spelling came the pronunciation, "Jehovah."

Jerusalem council The first church council, which convened in Jerusalem around 49 C.E. to discuss the legitimacy and nature of Gentile SALVATION (Acts 15).

Jerusalem Talmud   See PALESTINIAN TALMUD.

Jerusalem temple   See TEMPLE.

Jesus Christ   Combination of the personal name and a title for Jesus of Nazareth. "Jesus," a common name during the Second Temple period, was the Greek form of the name "Joshua," with the meaning "Yahweh is salvation" or "Yahweh saves" (Matt. 1:21). "Christ" is a title (Acts 2:36), the English transliteration of *christos*, "anointed," the Greek translation of the Hebrew word for MESSIAH. See also CHALCEDONIAN, LOGOS, QUEST OF THE HISTORICAL JESUS, and TRINITY.

Jew   A member of the nation ISRAEL. "Jew" can also refer to a devotee of JUDAISM. The word derives from the name "JUDAH," a son of Jacob and a tribe of Israel.

Jewish   Of or relating to JUDIASM or the nation of ISRAEL. Also being a Jew, as in "I am Jewish." See also JEW.

Jewish Christian   A JEW who believes that Jesus was the MESSIAH, thereby making him or her a Christian. Also called a Messianic Jew.

Johannine   Written by or characteristic of the APOSTLE John, supposed author of 1, 2, and 3 John, Revelation, and the GOSPEL that bears his name.

Josiah's reforms   The religious revival initiated by Josiah, king of JUDAH (c. 640–c. 602 B.C.E.), following the discovery in the TEMPLE of the book of the LAW, presumably Deuteronomy (2 Kings 22–23).

jot   English designation for the smallest HEBREW letter (*yod*), which Jesus declared will not pass away from the MOSAIC LAW until everything is accomplished (Matt. 5:18).

Jubilee   In JUDAISM, every fiftieth year during which time the land was given rest and, if necessary, restored (along with other lost property) to its original owner who had perhaps fallen on hard times (Lev. 25:8–55). Also, slaves were freed and debts were cancelled in the Year of Jubilee.

Judah   One of Jacob's sons, or the tribe of ISRAEL that traced its ancestry to Judah. Also the land area apportioned to the tribe of Judah. During the period of the DIVIDED KINGDOM, the term referred to the SOUTHERN KINGDOM.

Judaism   The JEWISH religion.

Judaizer   Someone who taught that GENTILE Christians must observe JEWISH customs (especially CIRCUMCISION) in order to be considered legitimate Christians (Gal. 2:14).

judge   An individual raised up by God to deliver ISRAEL from enemy oppression (see Judg. 2:18–19; 3:10).

judgment seat of Christ   See BEMA SEAT.

jussive   In HEBREW, an IMPERFECT TENSE verb in the second or third PERSON that expresses the speaker's will. For example, in Psalm 96:11–12, the PSALMIST demands a glad response from creation: "Let the heavens rejoice."

justification   God's pronouncement of a believer as righteous (Rom. 4:25; 5:16, 18). In Protestant THEOLOGY, justification occurs at the moment of SALVATION, when RIGHTEOUSNESS is imputed instantaneously to the believer. This doctrine received much attention from Reformers during the sixteenth-century Protestant REFORMATION. See also IMPUTATION.

K

kairos Greek for time, meaning "occasion" or "appointed time."

kenosis Term used for the self-emptying of Jesus (Gk., *ekenosen* in Phil. 2:7, "he emptied"). Many explain the simultaneous coexistence of the human and the divine in Jesus by holding that Jesus voluntarily relinquished ("emptied himself of") some of his divine qualities when he became human, especially OMNIPRESENCE, OMNIPOTENCE, and OMNISCIENCE (Phil. 2:6–11).

kenoticism Teaching that emphasizes the KENOSIS (Gk., "emptying") of Christ.

kerygma Greek term meaning "proclamation," often used of the early church's declarations concerning Christ (Titus 1:3).

Kethib(h) See KETHIV.

Kethiv HEBREW, "that which is written." A term used of textual variants in the Hebrew Bible that are represented by the consonants written or printed in the text; an uncorrected word in the Hebrew text. See also QERE.

Kethiv-Qere HEBREW for "that which is written—that which is read." See KETHIV and QERE.

Ketubim HEBREW for "writings," designating the third main division of the Hebrew Bible, after the LAW and the PROPHETS.

The Ketubim is made up of Ruth, 1 and 2 Chronicles, Ezra, Nehemiah, Esther, Job, Psalms, Proverbs, Ecclesiastes, Song of Solomon, Lamentations, and Daniel. Also called the WRITINGS. See also TANAK.

Khirbet Qumran See QUMRAN.

King James Onlyism The belief that the King James Version of the Bible alone is authoritative. See also AUTHORIZED VERSION.

King James Version See AUTHORIZED VERSION.

King's Highway A heavily traveled, north-south trade route to the east of the Jordan River connecting Egypt to Arabia (Num. 20:17; 21:22).

kingdom of God A realm over which God reigns, often describing the era inaugurated by Jesus Christ in which good fortune and BLESSING are restored to the Jews and extended to include Gentiles (Mark 4:26–29; 10:14–25; Luke 10:9–11). The Synoptic Gospels record Jesus' frequent descriptions of this kingdom (e.g., Matt. 13:44–46), along with the conduct expected of its citizens (e.g., Matt. 18:1–4). The "kingdom of God" mentioned primarily in Mark and Luke is likely equivalent to Matthew's "kingdom of heaven."

kingdom of heaven See KINGDOM OF GOD.

kinsman-redeemer A male relative who, according to Old Testament LAW (Lev. 25:25), was given the first opportunity to buy back family property to protect his clan.

Khirbet Qumran The archaeological site where the DEAD SEA SCROLLS were discovered, usually called simply "QUMRAN."

Koheleth   See QOHELETH.

Koine Greek   The form of the GREEK language prominent from roughly the third century B.C.E. until the third century C.E. (Gk., *koine*, "common"). The New Testament was written in Koine Greek.

Koine text-type   See BYZANTINE TEXT-TYPE.

koinonia   Greek for "fellowship" or "sharing in common" (Acts 2:42; Gal. 2:9). See also FELLOWSHIP.

K

L

L According to some, a source—whether oral or written—that Luke used in composing his Gospel. Some use this designation simply to refer to Luke's unique material, without actually commenting on whether Luke used such a source. According to the Four Document Hypothesis, Mark, Q (a putative source of non-Markan material common to Matthew and Luke), M (Matthew's unique material), and L were used in the production of the SYN-OPTIC GOSPELS.

labial A speech sound pronounced with the lips.

laity Those not employed in vocational ministry; nonclergy. See also CLERGY.

lake of fire Final destination of the wicked, characterized by perpetual anguish. The lake of fire is the place of eternal condemnation for death, Hades, fallen angels, Satan, and anyone whose name has not been recorded in the book of life (Rev. 20:14–15).

Lamb of God New Testament title for Jesus, highlighting his sacrificial atonement for sins (John 1:29, 36; see also 1 Peter 1:19; Rev. 5:6–14). The title alludes to Old Testament sin offerings and, possibly, the Passover lamb.

lament An expression of grief or sorrow; a lamentation. Laments come in a variety of forms, such as psalms (2 Sam. 1:19–27) or poems (Lam. 1–4). See also LAMENT PSALM.

lament psalm A psalm in which a crisis is described and God's assistance is invoked (e.g., Pss. 74; 137). This is not lament in the traditional sense of lament for the dead, but a complaint psalm for the psalmist's difficult situation in life.

Last Supper The final Passover meal eaten by Jesus and his disciples on the night Jesus was betrayed and subsequently executed. See also COMMUNION.

Late Bronze Age The era from 1550 to 1200 B.C.E.

Latin Bible See VULGATE.

Latter Prophets The Old Testament books of Isaiah through Malachi (except Lamentations and Daniel), or the prophets themselves. The LATTER PROPHETS, together with the Former Prophets, constitute the second division of the Hebrew Bible, designated as the PROPHETS.

Law The first division of the Hebrew Bible—Genesis through Deuteronomy—followed by the PROPHETS and the WRITINGS; the TORAH. Also designates the body of requirements recorded in Exodus through Deuteronomy and encapsulated in the TEN COMMANDMENTS (Ex. 20:1–17); the MOSAIC LAW.

laying on of hands Gesture that variously accompanies commissioning (Acts 6:6; 13:13), healing (Mark 5:21–24), sacrifice (Lev. 1:2–4), or the coming of the Holy Spirit (Acts 8:14–17; 19:6).

leaven Yeast or a yeastlike substance used to cause fermentation in dough. The use of leaven was forbidden in certain offerings (Lev. 2:11; 7:12; 8:2; Num. 6:15), and UNLEAVENED BREAD was obligatory in the FEAST OF PASSOVER meals to remind the Israelites of their hasty departure from Egypt. Because of the enigmatic way that leaven spread and changed the form of dough, it was widely used as a metaphor for sin in rabbinic literature and in the New Testament (Matt. 16:6, 11; Mark 8:15; Luke 12:1; 1 Cor. 5:6–7), though it is also used in a positive sense of the growth of the kingdom of heaven (Matt. 13:33).

lectionary Ancient manual containing portions of Scripture (i.e., "lections") that were read during SYNAGOGUE or church worship, or in other ceremonies. Thus ancient lectionaries provide evidence for TEXT-CRITICAL studies.

legalism Strict obedience to a set of laws. In the Gospels, legalism is associated with the PHARISEES; in several of Paul's letters, with the JUDAIZERS.

legend In biblical studies, a story that disproportionately exalts its main character. In this sense, legends are not necessarily fictitious, as the word commonly suggests. See also FABLE.

Leningrad Codex See CODEX LENINGRAD.

Lent Designation for the forty days preceding EASTER (excluding Sundays), during which time many Christians fast or otherwise abstain from liberties of their own choosing. The custom likely derived from baptismal candidates in the early church who fasted for forty days in preparation for the baptismal celebration held annually on Easter.

leprosy Broad term encompassing a number of skin diseases and infections. The Old Testament declared those with leprosy as unclean (Lev. 13–14), which sometimes indicated God's judgment (Num. 12:10; 2 Kings 5:27; 15:5).

Levant Of or pertaining to the land that borders the eastern shore of the Mediterranean Sea, or the land itself.

leviathan A powerful creature (perhaps mythical) whose precise identity is disputed (Job 41:1; Ps. 104:26; Isa. 27:1). Suggestions include a whale, dolphin, crocodile, or mythical DRAGON.

levir HEBREW for "brother-in-law." Describes the man who assumes the responsibilities of the LEVIRITE MARRIAGE (not always a brother-in-law).

levirite marriage A marriage union between a widow with no heir and one of her brothers-in-law, as prescribed by Old Testament law (see Deut. 25:5). See also KINSMAN-REDEEMER.

Levitical priesthood The office of mediation between God and Israel comprised of Levitical priests, descendants of Levi, son of Jacob. See also AARONIC PRIESTHOOD.

lex talionis Latin for "law of the talon" (Ex. 21:23–25; Lev. 24:19–20; Deut. 19:21). This law of retaliation demanded exact reciprocal justice (an eye for an eye, a tooth for a tooth, etc.), a principle Jesus later refuted (Matt. 5:38–42).

libation See DRINK OFFERING.

liberation theology A twentieth-century movement that sought release for those less-fortunate from political, social, or economic oppression. Liberation theologians place special emphasis on God's preference in Scripture for the poor and the powerless, and thus for minorities and citizens of Third World countries today.

limited atonement One of the five points of CALVINISM (the "L" in TULIP), which states that the blood of Christ is effective for the sins of the ELECT only (see Matt. 20:28; Mark 10:45). Advocates of limited atonement argue that while the blood of Christ is capable of cleansing the sins of all humanity, for it to do so would be superfluous. Also called particular redemption. See also CALVINISM, FIVE POINTS OF.

lingua franca   Literally, "language of the Franks" (Lat.). A common language spoken throughout a region or empire among peoples with varying native languages. GREEK was the lingua franca in PALESTINE at the time of Christ.

linguistic analysis   Study of a writer's vocabulary, grammar, and SYNTAX. Among other things, linguistic analysis is used in determining AUTHORSHIP and date of certain texts.

lintel   A horizontal beam forming the top portion of a doorway (Ex. 12:7, 22–23).

literary criticism   The study of a book's AUTHORSHIP, date, GENRE, structure, themes, sources, and so on. Also called HIGHER CRITICISM.

litotes   A statement framed negatively that is actually a positive affirmation, as in "I am not ashamed of the gospel" (Rom. 1:16), with the meaning, "I am bold and forthright in proclaiming the gospel."

liturgy   Worship forms characterized by ritual and formality, often incorporating creeds and responsive readings.

loanword   A word borrowed from another language. The essential meaning of a loanword is retained, but its spelling and pronunciation are usually modified to suit the adopting language. See also COGNATE.

local flood theory   The view that the GENESIS FLOOD was not global, but was limited to one geographical region inhabited in the time of Noah.

locative Of linguistic forms and constructions (usually in Greek rather than Hebrew) that denote things such as location, sphere, or destination. The locative is a separate CASE in the EIGHT-CASE SYSTEM.

logos GREEK term meaning "word, speech, reason." "Logos" has a rich pre-Christian heritage in philosophic and Jewish literature, including the Old Testament, from which John possibly drew when he used the term as a title for Jesus (John 1:1, 14; Rev. 19:13).

loincloth A man's undergarment worn around the waist next to the skin (Job 12:18). Also waistcloth.

Lord's Prayer, the Traditional name for Matthew 6:9–13, which begins, "Our Father in heaven, hallowed be your name" (see also Luke 11:2–4).

Lord's Supper See COMMUNION.

lordship salvation The view that people receive SALVATION not by putting faith in Jesus and nothing else (often termed "easy believism" or "cheap grace"; see James 2:19) but by REPENTANCE, which involves turning away from one's sins, and submission to Christ as Lord, including a subjection of one's will and a commitment to obey God. Likewise, this view holds that those who are genuine Christians will evidence a discernible change in character and behavior, otherwise his or her Christian confession is called into question.

lots, casting of A method of determining answers or making decisions by rolling stones of various shapes or colors (Prov. 18:18; Jonah 1:7; Luke 1:9; see also Prov. 16:33).

lower criticism See TEXTUAL CRITICISM.

Lucan   Variant spelling of LUKAN.

Lucian's recension   A deliberate modification of the Greek Old and New Testaments by Lucian of Antioch (d. c. 312 C.E.), characterized by conflation and smoothed-out readings. See also RECENSION.

Lukan   Written by or characteristic of Luke, the traditional author of the Gospel of Luke and Acts. Also Lukan.

LXX   See SEPTUAGINT.

lyre   A stringed instrument used in praise of God, often accompanied by the harp (Pss. 57:8; 81:2).

L

M

M According to some, a source—whether oral or written—that Matthew used in composing his Gospel. It evidently stands behind the portions that are not found in Mark or Luke (e.g., Matt. 13:44–46; 20:1–16). Some use this designation simply to refer to Matthew's unique material without actually commenting on whether Matthew used such a source. According to the Four Document Hypothesis, Mark, Q (a putative source of non-Markan material common to Matthew and Luke), M, and L (Luke's unique material) were used in the production of the SYNOPTIC GOSPELS.

Maccabean Revolt A Jewish military uprising from 167– 164 B.C.E., in which Judas Maccabeus led a guerilla army against the Syrians and their king, Antiochus IV Epiphanes. This was in response to widespread hellenization and religious persecution. Traditional worship was restored to the Jewish TEMPLE when it was cleansed and rededicated in 165/164, commemorated by the FEAST OF LIGHTS or Hanukkah (1 Macc. 4:36–59; 2 Macc. 10:1–8). Judas acquired the popular name "Maccabee" (probably with the meaning "hammer"); thus his family became known as MACCABEES.

Maccabees The name given to Judas ben Mattathias, his immediate family, and his descendants, probably derived from a word meaning "hammer," in accordance with the family's crushing military power in upholding the cause of Jewish independence during the MACCABEAN REVOLT. In Jewish literature the family members were also called Hasmoneans.

Magi The astrologers or "wise men" who, according to Matthew's Gospel, followed a star first to Jerusalem and then to Bethlehem to worship the child Jesus (Matt. 2:1–12, 16). The same Greek word also appears in Acts 13:6, 8, where it is usually translated "magician" or "sorcerer."

Magnificat The traditional name for Mary's song of praise in Luke 1:46–55, which begins, "My soul glorifies the Lord." The opening word of the Latin VERSION of this passage is *magnificat,* "exalt."

main clause In grammar, the CLAUSE that contains the MAIN VERB, to which other clauses are subordinate.

main verb In grammar, the principal or controlling VERB in a CLAUSE, contained in the MAIN CLAUSE, and to which other grammatical elements are subordinate.

major prophets The Hebrew spokesmen Isaiah, Jeremiah, and Ezekiel, or the Old Testament books that bear their names. The distinction between major and MINOR PROPHETS is based solely on the length of these books—these three books comprise approximately 20 percent of the Old Testament. Some use this term to refer to Isaiah to Daniel in contrast to the Minor Prophets, Hosea to Malachi.

Majoristic controversy A debate within German Lutheranism following the death of Martin Luther in 1546 over the relationship of good works to SALVATION. See also LORDSHIP SALVATION.

Majority Text Designation for most (a "majority") of the surviving New Testament manuscripts; these contain readings that are very similar to one another but together disagree with the earlier, presumably more reliable, manuscripts, which are fewer in number. This later form of the text (also known as the BYZANTINE TEXT-TYPE) is called the Majority Text; it provided the basis for the TEXTUS RECEPTUS and later the KING JAMES VERSION. Almost all New Testament scholars believe the Majority Text is the least reliable text form; and with the exception of the New King James Version, no modern translation of the New Testament relies solely on this text-type.

majuscule   A large, capital letter used in the production of manuscripts (called uncials), principally from the second to the eighth century. See also UNCIAL.

makarism   Another name for a BLESSING or "BEATITUDE," derived from the Greek word that appears repeatedly in Matthew 5:3–11, *makarios* ("blessed").

mammon   Wealth or possessions. The word entered the English language through TRANSLITERATION from Greek, but it is somewhat obsolete today (see Matt. 6:24; Luke 16:9–13).

man, new   See NEW MAN.

Man, Son of   See SON OF MAN.

manducation   The view of COMMUNION in which the bread is believed to be transformed into the actual body of Christ and thus is eaten in the Lord's Supper (Lat., *manducatio*, "eating"). See TRANSUBSTANTIATION.

Manichaeism   A religious movement founded by Mani (c. 216 C.E.), a self-proclaimed APOSTLE, which combined elements from GNOSTICISM, Buddhism, and the Jewish-Christian sect of the Elkesaites in which he had been raised.

M

143

manna   According to Exodus 16, a breadlike substance that God provided for the Israelites to eat when they were wandering in the wilderness, which covered the ground like the dew (v. 14) and tasted sweet like honey (v. 31). Unsure of what it was at first, the Israelites named it "manna" (Hebrew for "What is it?"; v. 15). Some have tried to find an explanation for manna in nature (e.g., secretions from certain trees and plants in the Near East), although the accounts in Exodus 16:8–36 and Numbers 11:4–9 present God's provision of manna as a miraculous occurrence. John's Gospel presents Jesus, the bread of life, as immeasurably superior to the manna that the Israelites ate (6:25–58).

mantic   Related to PROPHECY.

manuscript   A text written or copied by hand. Since no original biblical manuscripts survive and the thousands of copies and fragments of copies we have contain errors, scholars attempt to reconstruct the ORIGINAL text through the science of TEXTUAL CRITICISM.

maqqeph   In HEBREW, a horizontal stroke similar to a hyphen that joins two or more words; these linked words are associated in meaning and are read together; that is, they are pronounced as if one word (often called a CONSTRUCT STATE). A word before a maqqeph becomes proclitic (i.e., it loses its accent).

maranatha   An ARAMAIC expression transliterated into Greek in 1 Corinthians 16:22. Because biblical manuscripts did not include spaces between words, it could either be a prayer (*marana tha*, "[Our] Lord come!") or a statement (*maran atha*, "[Our] Lord has come").

Marcion   An individual who attended the church in Rome until his EXCOMMUNICATION in 144 C.E., whereupon he founded his own church and taught doctrines labeled as heretical by almost all the prominent patristic writers. His ideas, largely shaped by GNOSTICISM, included a radical dichotomy between the Old Testament, with its harsh view of God the Creator and Judge, and the New Testament, with its kind view of God who sent Jesus to free humankind from bondage to the harsh God. Marcion rejected the Old Testament and any portion of the New apparently influenced by it. He believed that only the APOSTLE Paul correctly understood Jesus' teaching.

Marduk Principal DEITY of Babylon, who in the creation story *ENUMA ELISH* defeats Tiamat, becoming the head of the divine assembly (see Jer. 50:2).

marginal Massorah See MASORAH MAGNA and MASORAH PARVA.

Mari texts/tablets Approximately 20,000 tablets, written mostly in AKKADIAN, found at the ancient site of Mari on the middle Euphrates in MESOPOTAMIA and dating from the latter half of the eighteenth century B.C.E. These documents shed light on the cultural background of the PATRIARCH period.

Mariolatry Worship of Mary, the mother of Jesus. In the Roman Catholic tradition, only God should be worshiped, but Mary ought to receive special veneration or reverence.

Mariology Teaching about Mary, the mother of Jesus, particularly in the Roman Catholic Church.

mark of Cain After Cain murdered Abel, a visible sign that God placed on Cain to prevent others from avenging Abel's death (Gen. 4:15).

mark of the beast In the book of Revelation, a visible sign that the beast (i.e., the ANTICHRIST; Rev. 13:16–17) places on the foreheads or right hands of unbelievers. Those who do not receive the mark are prohibited from making purchases.

Markan Written by or characteristic of Mark (i.e., John Mark), the alleged author of the Gospel that bears his name.

Markan priority/hypothesis The notion that Mark was the first Gospel to be written, especially among the SYNOPTIC GOSPELS (Matthew, Mark, and Luke), and that Mark was used by the others as a source. A minority of scholars have proposed that Matthew was first (see MATTHEAN PRIORITY/HYPOTHESIS) and was used as a source by the others. See also SYNOPTIC PROBLEM.

martyr Someone who witnesses to others by dying for his or her beliefs. The word (*martyria*, "testimony") originally referred to verbal testimony, but since many early Christians were executed for their faith, the term came to signify those who actually died for their faith (see Acts 1:8; 2:32; 22:15; Rev. 17:6).

martyrdom The act of dying for one's faith—being a MARTYR.

masculine In Greek, Hebrew, and Aramaic, nouns and other words are either masculine, feminine, or (in Greek only) neuter. Other words will agree in gender with those that they modify.

mashal The HEBREW term that, in the plural, designates the book of Proverbs (appearing in 1:1, 6; 10:1; 25:1; see also Eccl. 12:9; Ezek. 16:44; 18:2); similarly, a Hebrew term denoting any proverb or pithy saying in which things are compared (Heb., "represent, compare").

maskil A term of uncertain meaning that appears in the titles of several psalms (Pss. 32; 42; 44–45; 52–55; 74; 78; 88–89; 142), likely designating either something about the content of the psalm (some have suggested that it indicates the psalm is about wisdom) or the way it was supposed to be performed musically.

Masorah   A system of textual notes and signs developed by the MASORETES in Old Testament MANUSCRIPT production in order to ensure that the biblical text would be transcribed exactly and pronounced correctly when read aloud (Heb., "tradition"). Different Masoretic systems were developed during the Middle Ages by Jewish scholars in different regions (i.e., the Palestinian, Babylonian, and Tiberian Masorah). Eventually the Tiberian Masorah became dominant and was accepted as authoritative. The Masorah has ensured accurate transmission of the Hebrew Bible since the early Middle Ages. Plural, Masorot. Also Massorah.

Masorah finalis   "Final *MASORAH*." Masoretic notations that appear at the end of Old Testament books, providing information such as the number of verses, the middle point of the book, and so on.

Masorah magna   "Large *MASORAH*." Masoretic notes written in the margins and at the ends of Old Testament books with lists of particular word forms, the locations of certain words, as well as unique forms.

Masorah parva   "Small *MASORAH*." Short Masoretic notes and abbreviations written in the margins of manuscripts, which identify the external form of the text, such as unusual spellings, word frequency totals, and so on.

Masoretes   Jewish scholars who, in an effort to ensure the accurate transmission and pronunciation of the Old Testament text, developed a system of textual notes and signs. The Masoretes did most of their work in the second half of the first millennium C.E.

M

Masoretic Text   The Old Testament text, supplied with vowel points and preserved by Jewish scholars (the MASORETES) during the second half of the first millennium C.E. (abbreviated MT).

matres lectionis   The HEBREW letters *he*, *waw*, and *yod*, which represent long vowels in an unpointed text of the Hebrew Bible (Heb., "mothers of reading"). Also called fulcra or vowel letters. Singular is *mater lectionis*.

matriarch   Generally, a woman who rules a CLAN or tribe. The term is also used of the female ancestors of Israel, who were wives of the patriarchs: Sarah, Rebekah, Leah, and Rachel.

Matthean priority/hypothesis   The notion that Matthew was the first Gospel to be written, especially among the SYNOPTIC GOSPELS (Matthew, Mark, and Luke), and may have been used as a source by the other Evangelists. Most scholars hold that Mark was written first (see MARKAN PRIORITY/HYPOTHESIS). See also SYNOPTIC PROBLEM and GRIESBACH HYPOTHESIS.

matzah   The UNLEAVENED BREAD eaten during the FEAST OF PASSOVER. Also spelled matzo.

maximalist   Designation for fundamentalist and conservative scholars who hold that the biblical accounts of history are largely, if not entirely, true, containing a "maximum" amount of straightforward historical information. See also MINIMALIST.

mediation   The bringing together of warring parties for RECONCILIATION.

Megillah   Singular of MEGILLOTH. It commonly refers to the book of Esther, which was read at the FEAST OF PURIM.

Megilloth   A term used to designate the five Old Testament books that were read at the religious festivals: Song of Songs

(Passover), Ruth (Pentecost), Lamentations (the ninth of Ab), Ecclesiastes (Feast of Tabernacles), and Esther (Purim). The term is from the Hebrew word for "scroll." Also spelled Megillot.

meiosis A literary feature involving understatement for rhetorical effect. For example, "It is not right to take the children's bread and toss it to their dogs" (Matt. 15:26). See also LITOTES.

Melqart The patron DEITY of Tyre in Phoenicia, associated with navigation and the establishment of Phoenician colonies. Some scholars think Melqart was thus the "BAAL" that Jezebel, the Phoenician princess of Tyre and wife of Ahab, introduced to Samaria.

memorial view of Communion Usually associated with Ulrich Zwingli (1484–1531), the view of the Lord's Supper that holds that it is merely a commemoration, as opposed to views that adhere to either TRANSUBSTANTIATION or CONSUBSTANTIATION. See also COMMUNION.

menorah Hebrew for "lampstand." This seven-branched candelabrum, described in Exodus 25:31–40; 37:17–24, was kept in the Holy Place of the temple and has been used as a symbol of JUDAISM from ancient times.

M

mercy Treatment of others that is characterized by kindness, compassion, and an inclination to forgive. In the Bible, God is described as merciful (Ex. 34:6; Isa. 63:9; Luke 1:50), particularly in providing SALVATION (Eph. 2:4; Titus 3:5). Likewise, God's people are told to be merciful (Matt. 5:7; 18:33).

mercy seat The golden lid placed on top of the ARK of the covenant (see Ex. 25:17–22; Heb. 9:5), with two CHERUBIM facing each other and with wings spread upward. Animal's blood was poured or sprinkled on top of the mercy seat for the ATONEMENT of sins. Some versions translate this as "atonement cover."

Merenptah Stele   See MERNEPTAH STELE.

merism   In literature, the juxtaposition of two elements that represent two extremes in order to denote everything in between. "In the beginning God created the heavens and the earth" (Gen. 1:1); "If I speak in the tongues of men and of angels" (1 Cor. 13:1).

merit of Christ   A term used in THEOLOGY to speak of the sufficiency of Christ's sacrifice for sin.

Merneptah Stele   An Egyptian victory inscription that describes a military campaign of Merneptah, pharaoh of Egypt who reigned from 1212 to 1202 B.C.E., against peoples in Libya and PALESTINE, including, recorded (in all likelihood) for the first time in history, Israel. Sometimes called the Israel Stele. Also Merenptah.

Mesopotamia   The geographical region between the Tigris and Euphrates Rivers. The term comes from two Greek words meaning "between the rivers."

Messiah   In Old Testament times a person set apart for a divinely appointed office, such as a king or a priest, was anointed with oil in a sacred rite. The word Messiah is a TRANSLITERATION of the Hebrew word "anointed" and was translated into Greek as *Christos* (also meaning "anointed"). In time the term came to refer specifically to the expected king who would deliver God's people, judge the wicked, and usher in God's kingdom. See also CHRIST.

messianic Jew   See JEWISH CHRISTIAN.

messianic psalm   Biblical psalm that is thought to speak prophetically of the coming MESSIAH (e.g., Pss. 2; 22; 118).

messianic secret   A term used to explain the phenomenon found in the Gospels—especially Mark's Gospel—in which Jesus commands people not to tell anyone who he is (see Mark 1:34, 43–44; 5:43; 8:30; 9:9). Some have suggested that Jesus never actually required secrecy and that this was Mark's invention to explain how Jesus was proclaimed as MESSIAH even though he never made this claim.

metalanguage The words—frequently technical terms ("jargon")—used to speak about language (e.g., "adjective," "clause," "metaphor").

metanarrative Something that exists outside or "above" a narrative or some other text (Gk., *meta*, "above"), but which is nevertheless in a reader's consciousness.

metanoia The Greek word for REPENTANCE or change of mind.

metaphor A figure of speech in which a comparison is made that is not explicit, as in "The LORD is my rock, my fortress . . . my shield . . . my stronghold" (Ps. 18:2); "I am the good shepherd" (John 10:11). See also SIMILE.

metathesis In TEXTUAL CRITICISM, the transposition of letters, words, or phrases in the process of copying the biblical text; or the transposition of two letters or sounds in a single word (Gk., *meta*, "change," *tithemi*, "to place").

meter The patterns of accented and unaccented syllables in poetry that produce rhythm.

metheg In HEBREW, a short vertical stroke written under consonants indicating the precise pronunciation of words (marking things such as stress).

metonym See METONYMY.

metonymy   A figure of speech in which one thing is designated by mentioning something associated with it, as in "I did not come to bring peace, but a sword" (Matt. 10:34), in which "sword" refers to conflict (see also Rom. 5:9; Col. 1:16).

mezuzah   HEBREW word for "doorpost." The Israelites were told to write God's commands "on the doorframes of [their] houses" (Deut. 6:9). The term eventually signified a doorpost on which a biblical quotation was inscribed (normally the above passage from Deuteronomy), or a SCROLL with the passage (or the scroll's container). Plural, "mezuzot." See also LINTEL.

microevolution   See PROGRESSIVE CREATIONISM.

Middle Bronze Age   The era from 2300 to 1550 B.C.E.

middle deponent   See DEPONENT.

middle voice   In GREEK, the VOICE that is normally used of verbal action in which the subject acts upon itself or for its own benefit or is in some other way affected.

M

midrash   Jewish commentary on Scripture (Heb. "investigation"). Plural, midrashim.

midrashim   Plural of MIDRASH.

midtribulationism   The view that the church will go through the first half of the TRIBULATION period (lasting three and one half years) before being raptured. See also TRIBULATIONAL VIEWS.

Milcom   Patron DEITY of Ammon (1 Kings 11:5). Some believe that MOLECH is a variant form of this god's name.

millennial kingdom   See MILLENNIUM, THE.

Millennium, the   The one thousand-year reign of Christ that is spoken of in Revelation 20 (from *mille,* "thousand," *annus,* "year"). Although this exact length of time is only mentioned in this chapter, some feel that other parts of the Bible also describe this future period of unsurpassed peace and righteousness as Jesus rules over the earth. See also AMILLENNIALISM, POSTMILLENNIALISM, and PREMILLENNIALISM.

millo   A fortification of some kind (Heb., "filling") built by David, incorporated into the Jerusalem wall, and strengthened by subsequent kings.

minimalist   Designation for scholars who believe that the biblical stories are largely fictitious, containing minimal historical information. Often the term is applied only to the most radical of these scholars, who claim that there was no "Israelite" identity or religion prior to the Babylonian exile. See also MAXIMALIST.

minister   Someone who serves God; a technical term to refer to CLERGY, or more generally of anyone who "ministers."

ministry   Service rendered to God.

Minor Prophets   Designation for the twelve Old Testament books from Hosea to Malachi, termed "minor" because they are shorter relative to the other prophetic books.

minuscule   A MANUSCRIPT written in small letters run together like cursive letters. The letters themselves are also referred to as minuscules, in contrast to MAJUSCULE letters. Miniscule script became the norm for manuscript production after the ninth century. The majority of surviving New Testament manuscripts are written in minuscule script. See also CURSIVE.

miracle   Any divine action—often accomplished through a human mediator (Acts 19:11)—that is deemed extraordinary and

M

contrary to natural law. The miracles in the Bible are often performed to authenticate divine REVELATION (John 10:38) or so that onlookers would see God's power and marvel (Ex. 34:10; from Lat., *miraculum,* from *mirari,* "to wonder").

Mishnah An authoritative compilation of rabbinic oral traditions that developed within JUDAISM, passed on from one generation to the next and finally put into writing around 200 C.E. The Mishnah consists almost entirely of halakic material, that is, interpretations of the MOSAIC LAW and procedural matters. It became the basis for the TALMUD. See also GEMARA.

missions The church's efforts to evangelize non-Christians or serve others in the name of Christ. Missionary zeal usually derives its motivation from passages such as Matthew 28:18–20 and Acts 1:8.

mitzvah Biblical or rabbinical injunctions or commandments (Heb., "commandment"). Also used of good deeds—the human response to divine injunction. Plural, "mitzvot."

mixed marriage A marriage between people of different faiths. It can refer to people from different Christian denominations, especially Catholics and non-Catholics, or from entirely different religious traditions.

modal Pertaining to a verb's MOOD. This term is also used of nouns and other words to denote manner and similar ideas.

modalism A view that denies the ORTHODOX understanding of the TRINITY, asserting that one God was manifested at different times and in different ways (modes). A number of groups in the early church held modalistic views. See also PATRIPASSIANISM, SABELLIANISM, and MONARCHIANISM.

mode See MOOD.

modifier A word or clause that qualifies or specifies the meaning of another word or clause. Articles, adjectives, and adverbs, as well as other elements, can function as modifiers. See also MODIFY.

modify To qualify or specify the meaning of. For example, in the verse "In his right hand he held seven stars; and out of his mouth came a sharp double-edged sword" (Rev. 1:16), the adjectives "right," "seven," "sharp," and "double-edged" all modify their respective nouns.

Molech An Ammonite DEITY, whose worship sometimes involved human sacrifice (see Lev. 18:21; 20:2–5; 1 Kings 11:7; 2 Kings 23:10; Jer. 32:35).

Monarchianism An early view that said that Jesus was only divine in the sense that a power of influence, God's *dynamis,* rested on him.

money changers Banking officials who worked inside the TEMPLE precincts in ancient PALESTINE. Jesus drove them out of the temple, probably because their business practices were corrupt and did not honor God (Matt. 21:12; Mark 11:15; see also John 2:14–15).

monism The view that all things in nature are of one essence. In religion the term is somewhat equivalent to PANTHEISM, though in pantheism the essence of all things is divine.

monogenism The view that the human race originated from a single couple. Also called monogeny.

monogeny See MONOGENISM.

monolatry Worship of one DEITY, even though other deities may be acknowledged.

Monophysitism   A fifth-century Christological view that Christ did not have two natures but rather one (*monos*, "one," *physis*, "nature").

monotheism   Belief in the existence of only one god, as opposed to POLYTHEISM, belief in many gods.

Monothelitism   The view that taught that Christ lacked a human will but rather possessed only one (divine) will (from Greek *monos*, "one," *thelo*, "to wish, will, desire"). The Third Council of Constantinople (680 C.E.) asserted that in Christ there are not only two natures but also two wills, which operate harmoniously in one person.

Montanism   An apocalyptic movement initiated and led by Montanus, a converted PAGAN priest, in Phrygia (modern-day Turkey) in the second century C.E., which stressed the Spirit's endowment of prophets and prophetesses. There was also an emphasis on ASCETICISM and prophecies about the end of the world.

M

mood   In Greek, the feature of the VERB system that denotes the nature of the verbal action with regard to its actuality or potentiality. Mood pertains to whether verbs are commands, statements, prayers, or statements about how things might be or should be, among other things.

moral argument   An argument for the existence of a moral God based on the apparent existence of universal moral standards.

moral law   According to COVENANT THEOLOGY, the division of the MOSAIC LAW that deals with timeless moral principles (e.g., the Ten Commandments). Thus Christians are said to be obligated to keep the Old Testament moral law. See also CEREMONIAL LAW and CIVIL LAW.

morality An ideological system about right and wrong conduct, or simply, the rightness or wrongness of one's actions.

morphology The study of words with regard to how they are formed and inflected.

Mosaic Of or pertaining to Moses (e.g., MOSAIC LAW , Mosaic authorship).

Mosaic covenant Synonym for the MOSAIC LAW , with special reference to the fact that a COVENANT was made with God and Israel at Mount Sinai: "Now if you obey me fully and keep my covenant, then out of all nations you will be my treasured possession" (Ex. 19:5). Likewise the ARK, which contained the tablets inscribed with the TEN COMMANDMENTS, was called the "ark of the covenant" (Num. 10:33).

Mosaic law The body of laws given to God's people through Moses at Mount Sinai. The Mosaic law appears throughout most of the PENTATEUCH but is encapsulated in the TEN COMMAND-MENTS (Ex. 20:1–17).

Mosaic-Sinai tradition Term scholars use to designate the COVENANT at Mount Sinai (Ex. 19–20) and later events associated with it (e.g., the Shechem covenant ceremony in Josh. 24). The centerpiece of this covenant tradition is the tenet that Israel is under sworn obligation to YAHWEH to perform the stipulations (or "commandments") of the covenant. This term is often used in contrast with the Davidic-Zion tradition or with the Abrahamic tradition, both of which emphasize not Israel's obligations to Yahweh but rather Yahweh's obligation to keep promises he makes on Israel's behalf.

Most Holy Place See HOLY OF HOLIES.

M

motif A dominant or recurrent element or theme in a literary work or some other artistic expression.

Mount Zion See ZION.

movable *nu* In Greek, a letter *nu* that is placed at the end of certain words but does not affect their meanings.

MT See MASORETIC TEXT.

Muratorian Canon See MURATORIAN FRAGMENT.

Muratorian Fragment A fragmentary eighty-five-line MAN-USCRIPT normally dated to the late second century, discovered by Lodovico Antonio Muratori in the mid-eighteenth century, which contains the earliest surviving list of New Testament books that its author considered to be canonical. Termed the Muratorian Canon, the list excludes Hebrews, James, 1 and 2 Peter, and 3 John. See also CANON.

mystery cults Religions of the Greco-Roman world whose adherents claimed to be privy to secret teachings and initiation ceremonies, which gave them promise of immortality.

mysticism Unmediated union with and experience of the divine. Christian mysticism usually emphasizes prayer, meditation, adoration of God, and relating to God directly.

myth The term may refer to a FABLE or some other fictitious story. But in biblical studies the word refers to a literary form that speaks of the world beyond and things that are transcendent in this-worldly terms. Myth frequently has a moral lesson or says something about SALVATION.

M

nabi' The Hebrew word meaning "PROPHET," a person who speaks for God.

Nag Hammadi library An extensive cache of Gnostic documents from the fourth century, discovered at the village of Nag Hammadi in southern Egypt in the 1940s. The Nag Hammadi documents shed light on GNOSTICISM and its interaction with early Christianity.

narrative In literature, a recounting of events, usually in chronological order, which can be distinguished from exposition and dialogue.

narratology Study of NARRATIVE texts.

nativity From Latin, *nativitas,* "birth," the birth of Jesus.

natural headship The view of ORIGINAL SIN that asserts that Adam was humankind's "natural head," in whom all of humanity was present in germinal or seminal form, thereby participating in his SIN and rendering them blameworthy. This view is generally related to the traducianist view of the origin of the human SOUL (i.e., individual souls are propagated by parents). Also called realistic headship. See also TRADUCIANISM and FEDERAL HEADSHIP.

natural religion A religious perspective shaped by what can be known of God from creation and through human reason. The

Catholic tradition, since Aquinas (1225–1274), has emphasized the potential of natural religion. See Psalm 19:1–4; Acts 14:17; 17:22–31; Romans 1:18–32; 2:14–15.

natural revelation   God's revealing of his nature and character through natural means such as the creation or through human conscience (see Rom. 1:18–32). See also SPECIAL REVELATION.

natural sin   See ORIGINAL SIN.

nazirite vow   An oath taken by a person who wanted to be especially dedicated to God (Heb., "separated, consecrated"). The vow involved abstaining from alcohol, not cutting one's hair, and avoiding contact with corpses (see Num. 6:1–21; see also Acts 18:18).

near demonstrative   In grammar, a PRONOUN that specifies that something is relatively near to the speaker or writer, as with "this" and "these." The opposite of FAR DEMONSTRATIVE.

nebiʾim   The plural of NABIʾ, meaning PROPHET. The term can refer to the second division in the Old Testament, the PROPHETS. Also spelled *Neviʾim*.

N

negative   As an adjective, pertaining to negation. As a noun, the word is shorthand for NEGATIVE PARTICLE, a small word (usually) that negates clauses.

negative particle   A word that functions to negate a clause or carry similar meanings such as denial, disapproval, prohibition, and so on.

negative theology   See APOPHATIC THEOLOGY.

Negeb   In biblical times, the southern area of PALESTINE. However, the modern designation "Negev" refers to the area that extends roughly from Beersheba to Kadesh-barnea in the northern sector of the Sinai desert, which makes up the southernmost part of the modern state of Israel.

Neo-Babylonia   The Babylonian nation from 612 to 538 B.C.E., in contrast to OLD BABYLONIA.

neo-orthodoxy   A modern theological movement, often associated with Karl Barth (1886–1968) and Emil Brunner (1889–1966), that began in the early twentieth century as a reaction to nineteenth-century liberalism, but which does not comprise a complete return to ORTHODOXY. Typically neo-orthodoxy does not embrace the verbal INSPIRATION of the Bible, but rather the Bible becomes the Word of God when it touches someone personally. It also seeks to reinterpret REFORMATION concepts such as God's TRANSCENDENCE, humanity's DEPRAVITY, and the work of Christ. See also DIALECTICAL THEOLOGY.

Nephilim   According to Genesis 6:1–4, a race of people who were the offspring of heavenly (male) beings and human women. The former group, the "sons of God," are mentioned elsewhere in the Bible (Job 1:6; 2:1; Ps. 29:1; 82:6). The Nephilim mentioned in Numbers 13:33 may have been called such by analogy to this tradition.

neoplatonism   The reshaping of the ideas of Plato by Plotinus (c. 205–270 C.E.) and others. Neoplatonic teaching stressed that God is manifested to the world through emanations in such a way that resembles PANTHEISM.

Nestorianism   The view that the human and divine natures were not united in the one person of Christ but remained separate. This teaching was condemned in 431 C.E. at the Council of Ephesus. The name derives from Nestorius, BISHOP of Constantinople (d. 451).

neuter In Greek, nouns and other words are either MASCULINE, FEMININE, or neuter. Other words will agree in gender with those that they modify.

neutral text-type According to some scholars more than a hundred years ago, a fairly reliable form of the New Testament text with close affinities to the ALEXANDRIAN TEXT-TYPE. It has since been demonstrated that it is not distinct enough to be considered a separate TEXT-TYPE but is rather an earlier form of the Alexandrian text, referred to as the proto-Alexandrian text.

new birth See REGENERATION.

new creation See NEW SELF.

new exodus A literary theme of Isaiah 40–66 (DEUTERO-ISAIAH), based on the NARRATIVE of Exodus 11–15. The author anticipated the release of Judean refugees from BABYLONIAN CAPTIVITY in an event similar to Israel's divine deliverance from Egypt.

new heaven and earth A biblical MOTIF that speaks of the consummation of eschatological hope and the renewal of the cosmos (see Isa. 65:17; 66:22; 2 Peter 3:13; Rev. 21:1).

new man See NEW SELF.

new moon The beginning of the lunar cycle that marks a new month. See also FEAST OF TRUMPETS.

new self An expression that appears several times in Paul's writings, signifying the new person that is created as a result of regeneration (Eph. 4:24; Col. 3:10; see also 2 Cor. 5:17; cf. Eph. 2:15), as opposed to the OLD SELF. Some translations render the term "new man."

New Testament   The second part of the Christian Bible, containing twenty-seven books: Matthew to Revelation. TESTAMENT means "COVENANT" or "agreement." Abbreviated NT. See also OLD TESTAMENT.

New Testament Pseudepigrapha   A large collection of pseudonymous gospels, epistles, and apocalypses that were not considered authoritative by the early church and therefore were excluded from the New Testament CANON. Sometimes the term is used synonymously with New Testament APOCRYPHA. From *pseudos*, "false"; *epigrapho*, "to inscribe, write."

Nicene Creed   Statement of faith drafted at the Council of Nicea in 325 C.E. to counter the Arian teaching (see ARIANISM) about the TRINITY, specifically the Father and the Son having merely a "similar essence" (HOMOIOUSIOS) as opposed to the "same essence" (HOMOOUSIOS—the term adopted at Nicea).

niphal   A verbal pattern (i.e., conjugation) in HEBREW that typically contains the letter *nun*. A basic function of verbs in the niphal is to express REFLEXIVE action, in which the subject acts upon itself.

Noahic covenant   The COVENANT God made with Noah promising that a flood would never again destroy the world (Gen. 9:8–17). The rainbow is in this passage described as a sign of the covenant.

nomina sacra   Latin for "sacred names." In copying the biblical text scribes would often abbreviate certain words, such as "God," "Jesus," "Christ," "cross," and so on, by writing only a portion of their letters (sometimes only the first and last letters) along with a horizontal line above them to alert the reader.

nominative   In GREEK, the CASE that normally functions to indicate the grammatical subject of a sentence.

noncanonical Writings that did not become part of the biblical CANON. Also called extracanonical. See also APOCRYPHA.

northern kingdom The name given to the ten or eleven northern tribes of ISRAEL (all but JUDAH and Benjamin) who followed the north-south split of the united kingdom in 931 B.C.E. See also DIVIDED KINGDOM.

noun A word that represents a person, place, thing, quality, state, action, or idea.

noun phrase A NOUN with all its modifying words and the constructions of which the noun is a part.

number In grammar, number signifies whether a word refers to one or more persons or things.

Nunc Dimittis The prayer of Simeon in Luke 2:29–32, named after the first words of the Latin text.

Nuzi An ancient city of the sixteenth and fifteenth centuries B.C.E., located east of the Tigris River, from which a number of documents survive that describe marriage and inheritance customs parallel to those in the Old Testament's ancestral stories.

Nuzi texts Clay tablets discovered at the ancient site of NUZI on the upper Tigris River reflecting customs and laws of the mid-second millennium B.C.E.

O

oath formula A standardized speech expression involving a solemn promise, usually one in which the speaker invites calamity upon himself or herself if the promise is not fulfilled (e.g., "May God deal with me, be it ever so severely," in 2 Sam. 3:35; 19:13; 2 Kings 6:31; cf. also Gen. 14:22–23; 1 Kings 20:10; Ps. 7:45). In the Hebrew of Psalm 95:11 the single word "if" stands as shorthand for such an oath formula (lit., "If they enter my rest"). This abbreviated oath formula is a HEBRAISM that is carried over into New Testament quotations of Psalm 95:11 (Heb. 3:11; 4:3, 5; untranslated in many modern versions); it also occurs in Mark 8:12.

object A NOUN or similar word that either receives the action of a VERB or PARTICIPLE, or is governed by a PREPOSITION.

objective genitive In GREEK, a GENITIVE case word that appears in a construction with its HEAD NOUN and receives the action of the verbal notion implied by the head noun. For example, in the phrase "the fear of the Lord" (Acts 9:31) the word "Lord" is in the genitive, functioning in an objective sense: "fear *for the Lord.*"

oblique case In GREEK, any CASE other than the NOMINATIVE or VOCATIVE.

occasion In biblical studies, the situation or events that engendered the composition of a particular book of the Bible. For example, the occasion of 1 Corinthians is clearly spelled out—Paul is responding to an oral report (1:11) and a written letter (7:1) from the church at Corinth.

occasional Of biblical books, arising because of an identifiable situation or as a response to a particular need in the church. See OCCASION.

ode A poem or song (see Eph. 5:19; Col. 3:16).

offices of Christ Theologians regularly speak of the work of JESUS CHRIST in terms of his having three roles or offices: PROPHET, priest, and king. As a prophet Jesus speaks for God (John 15:15); as a priest he offers his body for sin and intercedes for his people (Heb. 7–9); as a king he rules over the church (1 Cor. 15:25).

oikonomia Greek for "economy," "administration," or "arrangement." In THEOLOGY the term refers to God's administration of history, especially with reference to his provision of SALVATION over the course of history through various stages. See Ephesians 1:10; 3:2, 9. See also DISPENSATION.

Old Babylonia The period from 2025 to 1595 B.C.E., during which time the Mesopotamian city-states became united under the reign of Hammurabi (1792–1750 B.C.E.). See also NEO-BABYLONIA.

old covenant See OLD TESTAMENT.

Old Latin In Old Testament studies, the earliest Latin translation of the Old Testament, which was based on the SEPTUAGINT. In New Testament TEXTUAL CRITICISM, a designation for a group of Latin manuscripts that represent a tradition separate from the VULGATE.

old man   See OLD SELF.

old nature   A term used to describe one's nature prior to REGENERATION. See also OLD SELF.

old self   An expression that appears several times in Paul's writings, signifying the preregenerate state—that which a believer *used to be* prior to conversion (see Rom. 6:6; Eph. 4:22; Col. 3:9). Some translations render the phrase "old man."

Old Testament   The collection of thirty-nine books, Genesis to Malachi, that constitutes the Hebrew Bible, the name presupposing a "New" Testament (thus it is a distinctively Christian term). In Roman Catholic and Greek Orthodox traditions, the Old Testament also includes the APOCRYPHA. Abbreviated OT. Sometimes called the old covenant. See also NEW TESTAMENT.

Old Testament Pseudepigrapha   The large, diverse collection of JEWISH and Hellenistic writings that predate the New Testament writings and were not included in the Old Testament CANON or in the APOCRYPHA.

Olivet   An alternate name for the Mount of Olives, derived from the Latin word for "olive grove," *olivetum* (see Acts 1:12).

Olivet discourse   Jesus' sermon, delivered from the Mount of Olives, in which he delineated signs of the end of the age (Matt. 24:3–25:46).

omega   The last letter of the GREEK alphabet, which denotes a long "o" sound. In the book of Revelation, it appears repeatedly in connection with ALPHA, the first letter of the alphabet (1:8; 21:6; 22:13), to describe God as "the First and the Last" (1:17; 2:8). See also ALPHA AND OMEGA.

omnipotence   God's ability to exercise his infinite power and do whatever he pleases according to his will (see Job 42:2; Matt. 19:26; Luke 1:37; 2 Cor. 6:18; Rev. 1:8; 4:8).

omnipresence   God's being present everywhere at once (see Ps. 139:7–12; Jer. 23:23–24; Acts 17:24–28).

omniscience   God's perfect knowledge of everything that is and can be (see Heb. 4:13).

one flesh   An expression used in Genesis 2:24 of intimacy in the marriage relationship. In the New Testament, the expression appears in quotations and allusions to this passage (Matt. 19:5–6; Mark 10:7–8; 1 Cor. 6:16; 15:39; Eph. 5:31).

only begotten   A translation of the Greek *monogenes*, which is used in the New Testament of God's Son, Jesus (John 1:14, 18; 3:16, 18; Heb. 11:17; 1 John 4:9). The term elsewhere means simply "only, unique" (e.g., of only children; Luke 7:12; 8:42; 9:38); in the references to Jesus it may not bear any more significance than this.

ontological   Related to being.

ontological argument   An argument for the existence of God that states that since a Perfect Being (i.e., God) can be conceived of, and since existence is a perfection itself, then it follows that that Perfect Being must exist ("ontological" is from two Gk. words, meaning "being" and "study of"). According to this argument, God holds the power of existence and has himself always existed. The ontological argument is traced to Anselm of Canterbury (1033–1109 C.E.). See also CLASSICAL APOLOGETICS.

open theism   The view that the SOVEREIGNTY OF GOD and his knowledge of the future are limited. Open theists claim to

OF BIBLE AND THEOLOGY WORDS

derive their beliefs from a literal reading of passages that suggest
God is controlled by human requests (e.g., Ex. 32:7–14). Also
called free-will theism or the open view of God.

Ophel   Jerusalem's southeastern hill (Heb., "swelling, mound")
on which the City of David was located (see 2 Sam. 5:9; 2 Chron.
27:3; 33:14); apparently equivalent to ZION.

optative   In GREEK, the MOOD that is used in prayers and
wishes and other similar instances. Verbs in the optative mood
denote action that is possible.

oracle   A prophetic utterance or a literary unit of prophetic
communication (Num. 24:3–4; Isa. 15:1) or a person who proph-
esies (Prov. 30:1; 31:1). Also refers to a place of worship—a shrine
or SANCTUARY where a person would normally receive messages
from God.

oral torah   According to Jewish tradition, the part of the
TORAH orally revealed and transmitted through memorization
until it was committed to writing in the MISHNAH. Thus the Mishnah is accorded the status of Torah. Also called oral law.

oral tradition   Any material that is passed orally from one
group or generation to another. Undoubtedly many parts of the
Old Testament were preserved in oral form before they were com-
posed. Likewise, before the Gospels were written, stories about
Jesus evidently were conveyed by word of mouth. See also FORM
CRITICISM, TRADITION CRITICISM.

Origen   A Christian theologian, apologist, and philosopher
who lived during the early third century (c. 185–c. 254) in Alexandria, Egypt, working primarily in biblical interpretation and TEX-
TUAL CRITICISM.

original In TEXTUAL CRITICISM, the very first manuscripts (called the AUTOGRAPHA), or any particular MANUSCRIPT when subsequent changes were made to it (i.e., sometimes a later scribe would cross out words or make notes in the margin).

original righteousness The condition of innocence in which Adam and Eve presumably existed prior to the FALL. In this sense they were "righteous" before God. See also ORIGINAL SIN.

original sin In THEOLOGY, the condition of sinfulness and alienation from God into which all people are born. Original sin is traced to the FALL of Adam and Eve (Rom. 5:12–21), humanity's first parents (Gen. 3), and is transmitted to all later generations so that infants are sinners by nature (Ps. 51:5). See also ORIGINAL RIGHTEOUSNESS.

orthodox Considered to be correct and proper because it is in accord with both the Scriptures and with accepted church doctrine and/or practice. See also ORTHODOXY.

orthodoxy That which is derived from or in accord with the official teachings and creedal declarations of the early church. Orthodoxy, meaning "right opinion," is the opposite of HERESY or heterodoxy. The term can also be used as shorthand for Eastern Orthodoxy.

O

orthopraxy From Greek meaning "right behavior." Specifically, it refers to proper behavior that flows out of proper belief (ORTHODOXY).

ostraca Pottery fragments that were sometimes used as writing material in the ancient Near East. Some biblical texts are preserved because they were inscribed on ostraca. The singular is ostracon.

overseer In the New Testament, the translation of the Greek word *episkopos*, signifying a church office whose qualifications are listed in 1 Timothy 3:1–7 and Titus 1:7–9. This same term is also translated "BISHOP," "elder," or "presbyter."

Oxford hypothesis   One solution to the SYNOPTIC PROBLEM, which proposes that Mark was written first, followed by Matthew and Luke, who independently of one another both used as sources Mark and Q, as well as other material termed "M" and "L." Also called the four-source hypothesis. See also MARKAN PRIORITY/HYPOTHESIS.

oxgoad   See GOAD.

oxymoron   A rhetorical device in which paradoxical elements are placed in close proximity, as in Romans 6:8: "Now if we died with Christ, we believe that we will also live with him."

Oxyrhynchus papyri   A large number of PAPYRUS fragments found at Oxyrhynchus in northern Egypt, including fragments of biblical texts. The papyri date from the second century B.C.E. to the seventh century C.E., but most of them date from the third and fourth century C.E.

O

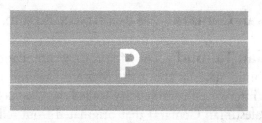

P According to the DOCUMENTARY HYPOTHESIS, the "Priestly" source in the PENTATEUCH, supposedly representing the latest of the literary strata (J-E-D-P). It consists of laws, editorial notes, and some stories.

paedobaptism The belief in or the practice of baptizing infants. It is practiced in Roman CATHOLICISM, Eastern Orthodoxy, and many Protestant denominations, going back at least to the third century. See also INFANT BAPTISM.

pagan A follower of a pagan religion (see PAGANISM). Commonly (and often pejoratively), one who is not a Christian.

paganism A general term that refers to any of the ancient polytheistic religions of the Greco-Roman world.

palal See PILEL.

paleography The study of ancient writing and documents, including making determinations about the dates of ancient texts.

Palestine The narrow strip of land that lies mainly between the Mediterranean Sea and the Sea of Galilee, the Jordan River, and the Dead Sea, in which most of the events described in the Bible took place. This land area is approximately 70 miles wide and 150 miles long.

Palestinian Gemara See PALESTINIAN TALMUD.

Palestinian Talmud The MISHNAH, a compilation of traditional rabbinic material about the MOSAIC LAW and Jewish customs, plus interwoven commentary (called the GEMARA; or in this
case the Palestinian Gemara) that originated from religious centers in Palestine. The Talmud is of dubious value for New Testament background because commentary was still being added
hundreds of years after the first century. Also called the Jerusalem
Talmud. See also BABYLONIAN TALMUD.

Palestinian text family A group of Hebrew manuscripts
and translations that share certain characteristics in their variations.

palimpsest A PARCHMENT from which an original text has been
scraped and the manuscript reused (Gk., "scrape again"). For example, underlying the twelfth-century text of CODEX EPHRAEMI, a
much more valuable fifth-century text includes more than half the
New Testament as well as some passages from the Old Testament.

palingenesis Rebirth or REGENERATION (from Greek, *palin*,
"again," and *genesis*, "birth").

Palm Sunday The Sunday prior to EASTER, which commemorates Jesus' entry into Jerusalem (John 12:13). Palm Sunday
marks the first day of Holy Week. See also TRIUMPHAL ENTRY.

pantheism The view that God is all and all is God, especially
natural elements and the forces of nature, as opposed to
MONOTHEISM and POLYTHEISM, which claim that God is distinct
from his creation. Or, the worship of all deities.

papacy, the The office of the pope in the Roman Catholic
tradition, with special reference to the jurisdiction and authority
of the position.

papyri   Plural of PAPYRUS.

papyrus   A writing material made from the plant by the same name. To make the writing surface, the fibrous insides of the stem of the plant were cut open and laid flat. For added strength, two layers of papyrus could be sandwiched together with the fibers running perpendicularly to one another.

parable   A short instructive story that contains an analogy. In the Synoptic Gospels Jesus frequently teaches in parables; some of the best known biblical passages are parables.

Paraclete   Transliteration of a Greek word, *parakletos,* meaning "helper, advocate." The term appears five times in the New Testament—four times in John's Gospel referring to the Holy Spirit (14:16, 26; 15:26; 16:7), once in 1 John 2:1 referring to Jesus.

paradox   A rhetorical feature involving a statement that is or seems self-contradictory or contrary to reason. See Matt. 5:3–12; Luke 18:14; 1 Cor. 1:25; Phil. 3:7.

paraenesis   A sermon or exhortation; or textual material that includes instruction, exhortation, or commands.

paraenetic   Pertaining to instruction, exhortation, or command.

parallel   A biblical passage that resembles another passage in terms of lexical similarity, literary quality, or subject matter.

parallelism   A prominent feature of Hebrew poetry, whereby the meaning of one line is repeated with synonymous terms in the next. Parallelism can take on different forms: one line can restate another, or state the opposite, or lead to a climax, and so on.

P

parallelomania Arbitrary or thoughtless use of parallels or alleged parallels between two texts in an effort to establish literary dependence.

paraphrase A rewording or TRANSLATION that conveys the sense of the original but that is not necessarily a word-for-word rendering.

parataxis The linking of clauses or phrases together without conjunctions that mark subordinate relationships; makes frequent use of "and." The opposite of HYPOTAXIS.

parchment Writing material made from animal skins. See also VELLUM.

parity covenant A treaty between two equal kings that makes them mutually responsible to one another according to the terms of the contract.

parochial, parochialism Term used of a narrowness of interests or views, or the religious tendency to treat the specifics of one's own limited society as if they were of ultimate and universal significance.

P

parousia Advent (from a Greek term meaning "presence" or "coming"). It is used as a technical term for the SECOND COMING of Jesus.

partial rapture In ESCHATOLOGY, the view that believers will not all be raptured simultaneously, but rather in a series of raptures as individual believers are ready. The partial rapture view is not widely held. See also RAPTURE.

participle A word that has characteristics of both a VERB and an ADJECTIVE.

particle A word whose primary characteristic pertains to how it functions grammatically rather than what it means.

particular redemption See LIMITED ATONEMENT.

particularism In THEOLOGY, the view that SALVATION will be enjoyed only by some, which involves personal choice, in contrast to UNIVERSALISM, the view that all people will be saved regardless of their individual responses to the GOSPEL. Or similarly, the view that salvation is restricted to a certain group, the ELECT, rather than offered to all.

paschal Of or related to PASSOVER, EASTER, or the suffering of Jesus. "Paschal" is the Greek transliteration of the Aramaic word for Passover. See also FEAST OF PASSOVER.

paschal lamb The lamb eaten at PASSOVER (Ex. 12; see also John 1:29; 1 Cor. 5:7). "Paschal" is the Greek transliteration of the Aramaic word for Passover. See also FEAST OF PASSOVER.

passibility Able to undergo change; similarly, able to suffer and experience pain. Theologians have debated whether God is passible or impassible, whether he can be affected, especially in suffering, or if he remains unchanged. See also IMPASSIBILITY.

passible See PASSIBILITY.

passion of Christ A term for Christ's suffering, particularly the CRUCIFIXION. Yet the term regularly includes all his sufferings leading up to and including the crucifixion.

passion week The final week of Christ's life, culminating in his "passion" when he suffered and died on the cross. See also PASSION OF CHRIST.

P

passive deponent See DEPONENT.

passive voice The VOICE that conveys that the subject is being affected by or is the receiver of the verbal action.

Passover The Lord's "passing over" houses that had been marked with the blood of a lamb, thereby sparing the lives of the firstborn children and animals inside from the final plague against the Egyptians (see Exodus 12:1–30). Also the commemoration of this event celebrated annually during the FEAST OF PASSOVER.

Pastoral Epistles The New Testament letters of 1 and 2 Timothy and Titus, so named because of the ecclesiological matters and the "pastoral" concern expressed throughout.

patriarch An ancient ancestor or "father" of the Jews (from the Greek word for "father"), especially Abraham, Isaac, and Jacob.

patrilineal Of or relating to a way of tracing one's lineage, which is through one's male ancestors exclusively.

Patripassianism The view that the Son's appearing was actually a manifestation of the Father in a different mode, who thus suffered on the cross in the death of Jesus (from Lat. *pater*, "father," and *passus*, "having suffered"). Also called theopassianism. See also MODALISM, MONARCHIANISM, SABELLIANISM.

patristic citation/evidence A biblical quotation or allusion that appears in a writing by an early church father. Patristic evidence is helpful in TEXTUAL CRITICISM. See also PATRISTIC ERA.

patristic era The period of several centuries following the writing of the New Testament, during which time the "Fathers," prominent church leaders, ministered, wrote, and formulated doctrine. The patristic era is usually thought of as extending to Gregory the Great (d. 604) or John of Damascus (d. 749).

patristics   Study of the PATRISTIC ERA, especially church leaders of this era.

Pauline   Of or related to Paul, his writings, his doctrinal emphases, his literary style, and so on.

Pauline corpus   All of the New Testament letters allegedly written by Paul, including the DEUTERO-PAULINE and PASTORAL EPISTLES.

Paulinism   An expression that is characteristically PAULINE.

pax Romana   Term used to describe the two centuries of relative political stability in the Roman Empire (means "Roman peace"), beginning with the reign of Augustus Caesar in 27 B.C.E. and drawing to a close after Marcus Aurelius became emperor in 161 C.E.

peace offering   A voluntary SACRIFICE of fat to the Lord, the meat of which could be eaten by the one bringing the sacrifice, but only if done so on the same day (Lev. 3; 7:11–21). Also called fellowship offering.

pealal   A rare HEBREW verbal pattern characterized by repetition of the last two RADICALS (i.e., ROOT letters).

peccability   In THEOLOGY, the capability of Jesus Christ to sin. The notion of Jesus' peccability or IMPECCABILITY is raised in the discussion of Jesus' temptations, whether they were genuine and in what sense.

pedobaptism   See PAEDOBAPTISM.

Pelagianism The views associated with the British monk Pelagius (c. 354–c. 415 C.E.), who emphasized human freedom and effort, arguing that God's grace is given relative to human merit. According to Pelagius, the sin of Adam affected only Adam, so humankind is free from the taint of ORIGINAL SIN. Late in life he debated Augustine (354–430). Pelagius's views were condemned at the Council of Ephesus (431).

penal-substitution theory of the atonement A view of the ATONEMENT that understands Christ's death as the perfect payment for sin—as a substitute he took the penalty due humankind, thus appeasing the wrath of God. See also SATISFACTION THEORY OF THE ATONEMENT.

Pentateuch The first five books of the Old Testament, Genesis through Deuteronomy, traditionally attributed to Moses. Also called the TORAH, the LAW, or the Book of Moses (Gk., "five," and *teuchos*, "tool, book").

Pentecost An agricultural festival, celebrated fifty days after the FEAST OF PASSOVER, which entailed presentation of the FIRSTFRUITS of the harvest to God. Also called the FEAST OF WEEKS. On Pentecost, fifty days after Christ's RESURRECTION, the Holy Spirit was poured out on the church (see Acts 2). From the Greek word for "fifty."

perfect tense In Hebrew, a verbal inflection that frequently conveys completed action. In Greek, the verb TENSE that frequently denotes verbal action that has been completed in the past but that has present results.

pericope A paragraph, literary unit, or otherwise discrete section of writing, frequently the focus of EXEGESIS. Plural, pericopae. See also DISCOURSE ANALYSIS.

pericope adulterae   John 7:53–8:11, missing from a large number of early and diverse witnesses. Also called the *pericope de adultera*.

periphrasis   See CIRCUMLOCUTION.

periphrastic   Indirect; roundabout. See CIRCUMLOCUTION.

perseverance of the saints   One of the five points of CALVINISM (the "P" in TULIP), which states that God will preserve for himself until GLORIFICATION those who are genuinely his (i.e., the ELECT). See also CALVINISM, FIVE POINTS OF.

Persia   Ancient Near Eastern empire that rose to power after conquering the Babylonians and flourished from the late sixth to the late fourth century B.C.E. (Ezra 6:14; 9:9; Dan. 5:28; 8:20; 10:13).

Persian period   Period of time approximating the dominance of PERSIA in the ancient world: 550–330 B.C.E.

person   The feature of verbs and pronouns that distinguishes speakers (first person), addressees (second person), and persons or things spoken of (third person).

personal pronoun   A PRONOUN that replaces a NOUN that refers to a person.

Perushim   Hebrew, "Pharisees." See PHARISEES.

Pesach   See FEAST OF PASSOVER.

pesher   A type of Jewish interpretation of Scripture that emphasized present-day fulfillment. Some of the DEAD SEA SCROLLS are called pesherim, the plural of pesher.

P

Peshitta The standard version of the Syriac Bible (as the VUL-GATE was in Latin), which was produced in the early fifth century and contained only twenty-two books in the New Testament.

Petersburg Codex A Hebrew MANUSCRIPT dating from around 916 C.E. that contains the LATTER PROPHETS.

petition A request or prayer, whether directed toward people or God (see Est. 5:6–8; Phil. 4:6).

Petrine Of or related to Peter, his writings, his doctrinal emphases, his literary style, and so on.

Pharisees A Jewish sect that probably originated during the Maccabean period and emphasized strict adherence to the Old Testament's laws of purity. The Pharisees developed elaborate interpretations of the MOSAIC LAW, such as those found in the MISHNAH. They believed in the existence of angels, the RESURRECTION, and the coming of a MESSIAH. See also SADDUCEES.

Philo A first-century Jewish philosopher who lived and wrote in Alexandria, Egypt.

philology The study of the relationship of languages and the evolution of language over time. Sometimes called comparative philology or linguistics, or historical linguistics.

Phoenicians Greek term used of the Canaanites of the Iron Age who lived along the coast of the Levant (e.g., Sidon, Tyre, Byblos) and whose economy was derived from maritime commerce. They originally migrated there from other Mediterranean locations. Phoenician colonies such as Carthage survived well into the Roman period, preserving archaic traits of Canaanite culture (including religion and language). Many aspects of Israelite culture were essentially Phoenician.

phonetics The study of speech sounds in language—their physical aspects and how they are produced and perceived.

phonology The study of speech sounds, sound changes, and the intricate systems and patterns in language.

phylactery A small leather box containing parchment strips of Hebrew Scriptures, strapped to the foreheads or left arms of Jews in order to remind them of their duty to God. Today the Scriptures contained in these boxes are Exodus 13:1–10, 11–16; Deuteronomy 6:4–9; 11:13–21.

piel A verbal pattern (i.e., conjugation) in HEBREW that is characterized by the doubling of the second RADICAL (i.e., ROOT letter). Piel verbs frequently convey intensive or emphatic verbal action.

pilel A rare HEBREW verbal pattern, characterized by repetition of the third RADICAL (i.e., ROOT letter).

pilpel One of the rarer HEBREW verbal patterns (i.e., conjugations) distinguished by the repetition of the first and last RADICALS (i.e., ROOT letters), roughly corresponding to the piel in function.

plenary inspiration The view that divine INSPIRATION extends equally to all parts of the Bible.

Pliny the Elder Roman scholar of the first century C.E., best known for his *Natural History*, which contains commentary on the ESSENES as well as references to Judea that are of interest in New Testament background. Uncle of PLINY THE YOUNGER.

Pliny the Younger Roman governor of Asia Minor in the early second century C.E., whose official correspondence provides a valuable perspective on the Christian movement of that early time and place and the persecution of believers in Jesus. Nephew of PLINY THE ELDER.

pluperfect tense   In Greek, the TENSE that denotes an action that was completed in the past and whose results were also felt in the past (before the time of the speaker/writer). There are only about twenty verbs in the New Testament in the pluperfect tense (see John 4:8).

plural   Referring to more than one person or thing.

pneumatology   Theological study of the HOLY SPIRIT (Gk., *pneuma*, "spirit"), including his person, his role in the TRINITY, his activity in the lives of believers, and his bestowal of spiritual gifts for the church's ministry.

poal   A rare HEBREW verbal pattern.

poel   A rare HEBREW verbal pattern.

poetry   Writing characterized by imaginative and emotive imagery, especially metaphor and/or frequent rhythmic patterns, written not in paragraphs like PROSE but in lines of arbitrary length that are grouped as stanzas.

pointing   See VOWEL POINTING.

polal   A rare HEBREW verbal pattern.

polel   A rare HEBREW verbal pattern.

polpal   One of the more rare HEBREW verbal patterns distinguished by the repetition of the first and last RADICALS (i.e., ROOT letters), roughly corresponding to the PUAL in function.

polyglot Bible A book displaying the biblical text in three or more languages side by side. See also DIGLOT.

polysyndeton The superfluous repetition of a conjunction. It is the opposite of ASYNDETON.

polytheism Belief in multiple deities. See also MONOTHEISM.

polyvalence Multiplicity of meaning or significance in a text.

pontifical Of or related to the pope or the PAPACY. Similarly, the term is sometimes used of the HIGH PRIEST.

position In grammar, the occurrence of language elements placed in a particular order (i.e., word order).

positive degree Denoting attribution, as in "new" in "new wine must be poured into new wineskins" (Luke 5:38). This is in contrast to the COMPARATIVE DEGREE and SUPERLATIVE DEGREE.

positive theology See CATAPHATIC THEOLOGY.

possessive As an adjective, pertaining to ownership or possession. Or as a NOUN, shorthand for the possessive PRONOUN.

P

postexilic Pertaining to the period after the BABYLONIAN CAPTIVITY of JUDAH (c. 587/586–515 B.C.E.). See also PREEXILIC.

postmillennialism The view that Christ will return (see SECOND COMING) after the MILLENNIUM. This is in contrast to PREMILLENNIALISM, which holds that he will return before the Millennium, and AMILLENNIALISM, the view that the Millennium is entirely figurative and present. Postmillennialists tend to be optimistic about the future, holding that the kingdom of God is now spreading around the world by God's work through the church, which will to some extent lead to a Christianized world. This view normally interprets the "one thousand years" in Revelation 20 figuratively rather than as a literal period of time. See also ESCHATOLOGY and TRIBULATIONAL VIEWS.

postpositive   In Greek, a word that never occurs first in a clause.

posttribulationism   The view that the RAPTURE of the church will take place after the TRIBULATION. This is in contrast to PRETRIBULATIONISM, which states that believers will be "snatched away" (1 Thess. 4:17) just prior to the Tribulation, and MIDTRIBULATIONISM, which holds that believers will be taken out during the middle of the Tribulation. See also ESCHATOLOGY and TRIBULATION VIEWS.

praise   Adoration of God for who he is and what he does. In the book of Psalms, God is repeatedly described as worthy of praise (Pss. 66:2; 106:1; 113:1; 117:1; 150).

prayer   Speaking to God, whether in CONFESSION, INTERCESSION, PRAISE, thanksgiving, or supplication.

Prayer, the Lord's   See LORD'S PRAYER, THE.

P

preaching   The act of proclaiming or expounding a religious message, especially a message about Jesus Christ.

predestination   The doctrine that God, in conjunction with his FOREKNOWLEDGE (Rom. 8:29–30), decrees the eternal destiny of human beings, directing them and their circumstances accordingly (see Acts 4:28). The term is normally used in a positive sense, denoting God's ELECTION of individuals for SALVATION (Eph. 1:5, 11); however, it is sometimes used negatively (see DOUBLE PREDESTINATION).

predicate The part of a CLAUSE consisting of a VERB and often other components that complement the subject, expressing (predicating) something about it; the element or construction around which the sentence is organized.

preexilic Pertaining to the period of time prior to the BABYLONIAN CAPTIVITY of JUDAH (c. 587/586–515 B.C.E.). See also POSTEXILIC.

preexistence of Christ The belief that the Son of God existed as an eternal Person in the GODHEAD prior to his INCARNATION (see John 1:14; 1 Cor. 8:6; Col. 1:15–17; Heb. 1:1–2).

preexistence of souls The view that the souls of human beings exist prior to birth.

prefix A language element affixed to the front of a word, changing its meaning in some way.

pre-Masoretic text See PROTO-MASORETIC TEXT.

premillennialism The view that Christ will return (see SECOND COMING) before the MILLENNIUM, at which time he will set up a literal throne and reign on earth physically. This is in contrast to POSTMILLENNIALISM, which holds that he will return after the Millennium, and AMILLENNIALISM, the view that the Millennium is entirely figurative and present. Usually premillennialism is held in conjunction with PRETRIBULATIONISM, the view that the RAPTURE will occur prior to the TRIBULATION. Thus believers are removed just before God pours out judgment during the Tribulation; thereafter Christ directly inaugurates his literal one thousand-year reign characterized by unprecedented peace and righteousness. See also ESCHATOLOGY and TRIBULATIONAL VIEWS.

P

premonarchic period   The term referring to the time before the establishment of the Israelite monarchy of Saul and David (1200–1020 B.C.E.) when ancient ISRAEL was a twelve-tribe federation.

preposition   A word that governs a prepositional phrase, indicating the relationship between a NOUN or noun equivalent and another word.

presence, real   See REAL PRESENCE.

present tense   The TENSE that normally expresses progressive action occurring in the present.

presuppositional apologetics   A method of arguing for the existence of God that emphasizes the self-authenticating nature of Scripture. Thus presuppositional apologists assume that Christianity is true and reason from that point.

preterist view   A view of the book of Revelation that asserts that its prophecies are actually symbolic descriptions of events taking place at the time of the writer; thus they do not await any future fulfillment as such. See also FUTURISTIC VIEW and HISTORICIST VIEW.

preterition   Term used by Calvinists who are infralapsarian to indicate that not everyone is elected by God for salvation but some are "passed over" (Lat., *praeteritio*, "a passing by"). See also INFRALAPSARIANISM and REPROBATION.

pretribulationism   The view that the RAPTURE of the church will take place before the TRIBULATION, so that believers will be "caught up" (1 Thess. 4:17; the Lat. verb used here is *rapto*) and spared from God's wrath. This is in contrast to POSTTRIBULATIONISM, which states that believers will go through the Tribulation, though they will endure by God's grace, and MIDTRIBULATIONISM, which holds that believers will be taken out during the middle of the Tribulation. See also ESCHATOLOGY and TRIBULATIONAL VIEWS.

prevenient grace   According to certain theological systems, especially ARMINIANISM, grace that precedes conversion, extended to all people and rendering them capable of choosing God and faith in Christ. Theologies that speak of prevenient grace usually magnify FREE WILL, yet they maintain that God's prevenient grace comes before any decision on the part of individuals.

priest   In ancient Israel, someone who served as a mediator between Yahweh and the people, especially presiding over sacrifices and ceremonial worship. Priests were expected to be religious instructors and models of holiness. They also generally had some administrative and political duties. In the New Testament, Jesus is called the "great high priest" (Heb. 4:14), and believers are likewise called priests (1 Peter 2:5, 9).

Priestly source/writer   See P.

primacy of the pope   The Roman Catholic view that the pope is the primary BISHOP among all other bishops and the highest spiritual authority of the Christian church.

Prime Mover   According to Greek philosophical theory, a designation for the ultimate Cause or "Mover" who initially set the universe in motion. See also FIRST CAUSE.

primeval history   Designation for the material in Genesis 1–11, which narrates the beginnings of the world and of the nations before Israel's emergence.

primogeniture   The state of being the FIRSTBORN or the eldest child of the same parents; likewise, the right of inheritance of the firstborn, especially the firstborn male. The theme of primogeniture is particularly important in the book of Genesis. See also BIRTHRIGHT.

Prison Epistles The letters of Paul that claim to have been written while he was in prison: Ephesians (Eph. 3:1), Philippians (Phil. 1:7), Colossians (Col. 4:3), and Philemon (Philem. 1). Though 2 Timothy also has a similar claim (2 Tim. 1:8), it is grouped with the PASTORAL EPISTLES.

proclitic A word that does not have its own accent but depends on a closely related following word for accent. For example, in HEBREW, a word before a MAQQEPH becomes proclitic (i.e., it loses its accent).

profane To defile a holy thing, to make it impure by treating it with irreverence.

proglossolalia position The view that the gift of tongues, referred to as "glossolalia," is still operative in the church today, in contrast to CESSATIONISM, which holds that this gift has ceased. See also SPEAKING IN TONGUES.

progressive creationism The view that upholds CREATIONISM but allows for EVOLUTION on a small scale (sometimes referred to as "microevolution"); that is, God initially made creatures "according to their kinds" (see Gen. 1:21, 24), and biological mutations have occurred only within these groupings ("kinds" may or may not be synonymous with "species").

progressive dispensationalism More recent development within DISPENSATIONALISM that rejects any notion of the church age as a parenthesis in God's redemptive plan, seeing the church's receipt of covenant blessings, especially new covenant blessings (Jer. 31:31–34; Luke 22:20; 1 Cor. 11:25; Heb. 8:6–9:22), as in keeping with Old Testament promises that have been partially fulfilled or inaugurated—promises thought by traditional dispensationalists to be reserved exclusively for national Israel. Political-social benefits and spiritual blessings described in the Bible complement one another as part of God's unfolding plan; likewise the church today experiences the spiritual blessings that all the redeemed throughout history will share in spite of national identity. One of the outworkings of this approach is the affirmation that Jesus is presently sitting on David's throne (Isa. 9:7; Luke 1:32) as opposed to a generic throne.

progressive revelation Term used by theologians to describe the unfolding of God's redemptive program (see also DISPENSATIONALISM and SALVATION HISTORY) and the manner in which God revealed his nature and divine truths through history and through biblical writings over thousands of years (see John 1:17; Acts 17:30; Heb. 1:1–2). The concept of progressive revelation seeks to explain why theological concepts took shape and matured over the course of many years as evidenced in the Bible (e.g., the doctrine of the afterlife; the revelation of Jesus as the fulfillment of Israel's sacrificial system).

Promised Land Designation for the territory of CANAAN or PALESTINE, which was promised by God to Abraham and his posterity (Gen. 12; 17:8). See also ABRAHAMIC COVENANT.

P

pronoun A word that stands in place of a NOUN.

pronouncement story In GOSPEL studies, a brief NARRATIVE whose main point is a pronouncement by Jesus.

proof text A biblical passage brought forward to prove a point only, often with little explanation and without emphasis on the original historical setting, context, or meaning. The term can refer to New Testament writers quoting the Old Testament or to contemporary usage. This term can also be used as a verb.

proper noun   A noun that refers to a particular thing rather than a class, whether a person, place, event, group, organization, position, temporal name, and so on.

prophecy   Speaking on behalf of God, whether about contemporary situations or predictively (i.e., fulfilled prophecy). In the New Testament, prophecy is a SPIRITUAL GIFT for the edification of the church (Rom. 12:6; 1 Cor. 12:10; 14:22).

prophet   Name for divine spokespersons; a person who speaks for God (Ex. 7:1; Deut. 13:1; Jer. 1:5; Matt. 21:11; Luke 4:24). Likewise, a designation for a biblical book that records the words and deeds of God's messengers (i.e., Isaiah to Malachi, excluding Lamentations). Similarly, "false prophets" purport to speak for God but actually do not (Matt. 7:15; 24:11; 2 Peter 2:1; 1 John 4:1).

Prophets, the   The second division of the Hebrew Bible, along with the LAW (i.e., TORAH) and the WRITINGS. This grouping is often further subdivided: the FORMER PROPHETS include Joshua, Judges, 1 and 2 Samuel, and 1 and 2 Kings; the LATTER PROPHETS include Isaiah, Jeremiah, Ezekiel, and the twelve MINOR PROPHETS (Hosea–Malachi). Also called the *NEBI'IM*.

propitiation   The act of appeasing someone, especially a god, by SACRIFICE or some other means. In the New Testament, propitiation is accomplished through the death of Christ; God's wrath has been mollified so that he can forgive and accept sinners (see Rom. 3:25; 1 John 2:2; 4:10). See also EXPIATION.

prose   All forms of ordinary writing that lack the patterns of POETRY or the presentation of the text in stanzas. Prose is the language of everyday speech, as well as fiction.

proselytes   Gentiles who became "Jews," in the sense that they embraced Israelite MONOTHEISM, SYNAGOGUE worship, food and

SABBATH laws, and so on. Likewise males were circumcised according to the MOSAIC LAW.

protagonist   A literary term for the main character in a work. Opposite of ANTAGONIST.

protasis   The "if" CLAUSE of a CONDITIONAL SENTENCE (i.e., a sentence that contains an if-then construction), supplying a condition or hypothesis. The first clause in this verse is the protasis: "If there is no resurrection of the dead, then not even Christ has been raised" (1 Cor. 15:13). It is the counterpart of the APODOSIS.

Protestant Reformation   See REFORMATION, THE.

protoevangelium   Greek, "first gospel." The pronouncement in Genesis 3:15 that Eve's offspring would crush the serpent's head, supposedly a reference to Christ's defeat of sin and the DEVIL in his CRUCIFIXION and RESURRECTION.

proto-Lucian   A revision of the SEPTUAGINT in the second or first century B.C.E. that was brought into conformity with the Palestinian text family.

proto-Luke   A hypothetical document or draft believed by some to stand behind the Gospel of Luke.

proto-Mark   A hypothetical document or draft believed by some to stand behind the Gospel of Mark.

proto-Masoretic text   The Hebrew text form that was dominant in JUDAISM beginning in the second century C.E., providing the basis for most of the ancient translations and the primary text for the work of the MASORETES. Most of the biblical manuscripts discovered at QUMRAN represented this text family.

provenance   Place of origin. Determining a book's provenance is done by evaluating INTERNAL EVIDENCE (e.g., its own claims, linguistic features) and EXTERNAL EVIDENCE (e.g., early church writings).

proverb   See MASHAL.

psalm   A sacred song, especially one from the book of Psalms.

psalmist   One who composes a psalm. The term appears frequently in discussions of the individual biblical psalms, since their authors are often unnamed.

Psalter   Another name for the book of Psalms.

pseudepigraphic   Written under a false name. Also pseudonymous. See also OLD TESTAMENT PSEUDEPIGRAPHA and NEW TESTAMENT PSEUDEPIGRAPHA.

pseudonym   A fictitious name assumed for authoring a literary work; a pen name.

pseudonymity   The practice of authoring a literary work under a fictitious name. A large number of Jewish, Christian, and PAGAN writings from antiquity were pseudonymous.

Ptolemies   The Greek dynasty founded by Alexander the Great's general Ptolemy I Soter, son of Lagus. This dynasty ruled Egypt c. 323 to 30 B.C.E. The Ptolemies ruled Palestine from 301 to 198 B.C.E.

pual   A verbal pattern (i.e., conjugation) in HEBREW that, like the PIEL pattern, is characterized by the doubling of the second RADICAL (i.e., ROOT letter), and which frequently conveys verbal action in the PASSIVE VOICE.

publican   See TAX COLLECTOR.

pulal   A rare HEBREW verbal pattern (i.e., conjugation), characterized by repetition of the third RADICAL (i.e., ROOT letter).

punctiliar   Denoting verbal action that occurs instantaneously or at a point in time, as opposed to action that is progressive or ongoing; also action that is conceived of as a whole or as a point.

purgatory   According to Roman Catholic theology, an intermediate state or place prepared for those who die in a state of grace but who are not yet spiritually perfect, where their souls are purified from sin as they progress toward heaven. Roman Catholics appeal to tradition and to 2 Maccabees 12:43–45, as well as Matthew 12:32 ("anyone who speaks against the Holy Spirit will not be forgiven, either in this age or in the age to come"), suggesting that these imply that some sins will be forgiven in the afterlife. Protestants, however, contend that no further payment needs to be made for the sins of the elect (Mark 10:45; 1 Peter 3:18) and that SALVATION is not accomplished even in part by works (Gal. 3:1–14; Eph. 2:8–9).

Purim   See FEAST OF PURIM.

P

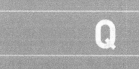

Q

Q In biblical criticism, a hypothetical source of Jesus' sayings that many scholars believe was used independently by Matthew and Luke in composing their Gospels (Q derives from the German word "Quelle," meaning "source"). Many scholars believe that both Matthew and Luke used Mark as a source (see Luke 1:1–4), but there is also a large amount of material that is common to Matthew and Luke but not found in Mark—this constitutes Q. A Q-hypothesis helps explain verbal agreement between Matthew and Luke (e.g., Matt. 3:7b–10 = Luke 3:7b–9), as well as similarity in the sequence of sayings.

qal A verbal pattern (i.e., conjugation) in Hebrew that is relatively simple and unencumbered (Heb., "light"). It denotes simple, active action. The qal pattern is sometimes abbreviated G, from the German "Grundstamm," meaning "basic stem."

qal wahomer One of the principles of Jewish biblical interpretation (called MIDRASH) adhered to by SCRIBES, which states that what applies in one case—a relatively minor case—certainly applies in a more important case (literally, this is a Heb. phrase meaning "light and heavy"). See also A FORTIORI.

qedeshim Males employed by the Jerusalem TEMPLE prior to JOSIAH'S REFORMS in the late seventh century B.C.E. Because the feminine form of the word usually means "prostitute," the qedeshim are often regarded as male prostitutes (1 Kings 14:24; 2 Kings 23:7).

Qere   Hebrew for "that which is read." A term used of textual variants in the Hebrew Bible that are represented by vowels printed in the text and consonants printed in the margin; a corrected word in the Hebrew text. See also KETHIV.

Qinah   An irregular meter pattern, with three accents to one line and two accents to the second (often marked as 3+2 or 3:2); this pattern normally expresses sadness (Heb., "LAMENT"), as in the book of Lamentations.

Qoheleth   A Hebrew term meaning literally "one who assembles" (usually translated "Teacher" or "Preacher"), which became the Hebrew title of the book of Ecclesiastes because its author refers to himself with this designation (see 1:1, 2, 12; 7:27; 12:8–10). Also Koheleth and Qohelet.

qualifier   A word that limits the meaning of another word or clause. Adjectives and adverbs are the most common qualifiers.

Quelle   See Q.

quest of the historical Jesus   The attempt to discover who Jesus truly was (the Jesus of history), in contrast to whom he has been proclaimed by the church (the Christ of faith). The term is often associated with scholarly historical-critical work of the nineteenth century and with the publication of Albert Schweitzer's (1875–1965) landmark book by this name. See also HISTORICAL JESUS.

Qumran   An archaeological site near the northwest shore of the Dead Sea, where the DEAD SEA SCROLLS were discovered and evidently where the sect that produced the scrolls—believed by many to be the ESSENES (a fringe Jewish group)—lived from the second century B.C.E. to the first century C.E. Also known as Khirbet Qumran.

Qumran scrolls   See DEAD SEA SCROLLS.

Q

rabbi   A respectful title for teachers or scholars (transliterated from Heb., "my master" or "my teacher"). In the first century, the term was used loosely of anyone who taught the MOSAIC LAW; later it referred more technically to experts or scholars. The term, almost always referring to Jesus, appears in Matthew, Mark, and especially John (see John 1:38, 49; 3:2; 9:2).

rabbinic Judaism   Jewish life and culture as expressed in RABBINIC LITERATURE.

rabbinic literature   Writings produced by rabbis, including the MISHNAH, the TOSEFTA, the TALMUDS (both the JERUSALEM TALMUD and the BABYLONIAN TALMUD), as well as commentary on Hebrew Scriptures (MIDRASH). See also RABBI.

Rabboni   A transliterated Aramaic term for "teacher" or "master," which is a strengthened form of the Hebrew "rabbi." It appears only in Mark 10:51 and John 20:16, both referring to Jesus.

radical   In HEBREW, another name for a ROOT letter. Hebrew words typically have three radicals.

radiocarbon dating   See CARBON DATING.

ransom, Christ's death as   The view that in the death of Christ a ransom payment was made to SATAN so that people in bondage to him could be delivered. This interpretation of Christ's death was articulated by ORIGEN (c. 185–c. 254), but Anselm's (c. 1033–1109) SATISFACTION THEORY OF THE ATONEMENT became dominant in the Middle Ages and afterward.

Rapture   According to PREMILLENNIALISM, the "snatching away" of believers to meet Christ in the air, based on 1 Thessalonians 4:17 (the Latin version of the NT uses the verb *rapto* here). According to PRETRIBULATIONISM, the Rapture will precede the Tribulation; believers will be taken physically from the earth and spared from God's wrath. According to POSTTRIBULATIONISM, the Rapture and the SECOND COMING will occur after the Tribulation. Others have proposed a midtribulational scheme, in which believers are raptured during the TRIBULATION. See also MIDTRIBULATIONISM.

rapture, partial   See PARTIAL RAPTURE.

Ras Shamra tablets   A collection of texts from the ancient city of UGARIT.

reader-response criticism   Discipline concerned with how readers respond to texts, especially the notion that new meanings are created when texts are encountered by readers.

reading   In TEXTUAL CRITICISM, the wording of a passage in a certain MANUSCRIPT compared to the same passage in another manuscript. Textual critics will say that one reading is likely or unlikely to be authentic, based on the reliability of the manuscript, the author's vocabulary and argument, and so on. See also EXTERNAL EVIDENCE, INTERNAL EVIDENCE, TEXTUAL CRITICISM, WITNESS.

real presence   A term used in Lutheran THEOLOGY of the belief that the true body and blood of Christ are genuinely present in COMMUNION. While Martin Luther denied TRANSUBSTANTIA-

TION, the Roman Catholic position that the eucharistic bread and wine are changed into the actual substance of Jesus' body and blood, he held that the body and blood of Christ are present "in, with, and under" the bread and wine (normally termed CONSUBSTANTIATION). See also MEMORIAL VIEW OF COMMUNION.

realistic headship   See NATURAL HEADSHIP.

realized eschatology   The view that future-referring biblical passages do not await a future realization but were fulfilled in biblical times, especially in the life and work of Jesus Christ. Thus the promise of a kingdom was obtained in the King himself—God's kingdom has come and is already accessible. Also known as the PRETERIST VIEW of ESCHATOLOGY.

reasoned eclecticism   In TEXTUAL CRITICISM, a method for determining the authenticity of readings. It takes into account EXTERNAL EVIDENCE and INTERNAL EVIDENCE equally. See also ECLECTICISM.

rebaptism   BAPTISM after one has already been baptized. Some churches do not recognize INFANT BAPTISM as legitimate; thus adult believers who were baptized as infants are enjoined to be rebaptized, usually by immersion as opposed to sprinkling.

recapitulation   A view of some early Christian theologians, particularly Irenaeus (c. 130–c. 200), that Christ as the last Adam (Rom. 5:12–19; 1 Cor. 15:45) restores the fallen creation.

Received Text   The name given to an edition of the Greek New Testament that was produced by Erasmus early in the sixteenth century and reproduced in Europe thereafter by several other publishers. An edition printed in 1633 contained a remark in its preface about this form of the Greek text being "commonly received." The translators of the King James Version relied on this

R

form of the text. Most scholars believe it is an inferior text form. Also called the TEXTUS RECEPTUS (or TR).

recension In TEXTUAL CRITICISM, a revision of an earlier passage of text or an entire document. Or this term can refer to a whole family of documents in light of that family's shared characteristics.

reconciliation God's gracious initiative through the death of Christ toward humankind in overcoming a relationship of hostility and alienation, restoring peaceful terms and receiving people to himself (2 Cor. 5:18–19). The Bible speaks of reconciliation in the Old Testament (e.g., the sacrificial system was essentially about reconciling sinners to God), but the idea is fully realized in the death of Christ and developed in Paul's THEOLOGY. According to Paul, unbelievers are God's "enemies" (Rom. 5:10–11) until they are justified by faith in Jesus Christ and reconciled to God. The Corinthian believers are described as God's "ambassadors" to the world, who proclaim the message of reconciliation (2 Cor. 5:18–20; see also Eph. 2:15–16; Col. 1:20–22).

redaction The process of modifying or editing a text; or the end result, a redacted text.

redaction criticism A method of biblical criticism that attempts to analyze the theological perspectives of the biblical writers by identifying how they compiled, edited, and reworked their sources in the composition of their own works. Redaction criticism is usually employed in the study of the PENTATEUCH and the GOSPELS.

redactor Someone who edits and/or collates documents; an editor. See also REDACTION.

Redaktionsgeschichte German term for "REDACTION CRITICISM."

R

redemption   Deliverance from bondage or legal obligation, especially by payment of a ransom. The Israelites' liberation from Egypt is repeatedly spoken of in terms of redemption throughout the Old Testament (Ex. 6:6; 15:13; Deut. 7:8; 9:26; 13:5; 15:15; 24:18). In the New Testament, believers are described as those who have been redeemed from slavery to SIN (Eph. 1:7; Col. 1:14; Titus 2:14), and from bondage to the MOSAIC LAW and its obligations (Gal. 3:13; 4:5). Redemption is also described as something for believers that awaits complete fulfillment at the return of Christ (Rom. 8:23; Eph. 1:14; 4:30). See also Mark 10:45; Rom. 3:24; 6:23; 1 Cor. 1:30; Heb. 9:12, 15; 1 Peter 1:18.

redemptive history   Translation of the German term *Heilsgeschichte*. See SALVATION HISTORY.

referent   The person or thing that is being referred to by a PRONOUN or CLAUSE.

reflexive   Denoting verbal ideas in which the subject and OBJECT (or, more precisely, the agent and goal) are the same person or thing, as in "whoever *exalts himself* will be humbled, and whoever *humbles himself* will be exalted" (Matt. 23:12).

Reformation, the   As a general term, the religious reform movement from the early fifteenth to the seventeenth century culminating in the establishment of Protestant churches throughout Europe. Reform efforts, the seeds of which can be traced back to the Middle Ages, were borne of discontent with the church and the PAPACY, especially abuses of power and practices that were considered unbiblical (e.g., INDULGENCES). The Reformation sparked debate about a number of key issues and doctrines, such as tradition, ORIGINAL SIN, JUSTIFICATION, and the sacraments—Protestants usually look to the Reformers for their understanding of these things. The Reformation is usually associated with the works and writings of two individuals in the sixteenth century, Martin Luther

R

(1483–1546) and John Calvin (1509–1564). Others ordinarily associated with the Reformation include Ulrich Zwingli (1484–1531), Philipp Melanchthon (1497–1560), and in England, Archbishop Thomas Cranmer (1489–1556) and Bishop Hugh Latimer (c. 1485–1555).

Reformed church   See REFORMED THEOLOGY.

Reformed theology   The theological tradition rooted in the teachings of the Reformers John Calvin (1509–1564) and Ulrich Zwingli (1484–1531), with an emphasis on God's SOVEREIGNTY in accomplishing SALVATION (ELECTION, PREDESTINATION, etc.). This term is sometimes used more broadly of other theological ideas that are associated with the REFORMATION; or as a general term to describe a theological approach contrasting with DISPENSATIONALISM. See also COVENANT THEOLOGY.

refuge, cities of   According to MOSAIC LAW, cities established in ISRAEL as places of asylum for those who killed someone unintentionally (see Num. 35). A person who accidentally killed someone was supposed to flee to the nearest city of refuge, where protection would be provided until there could be a public trial to determine the guilt or innocence of the offending party. In Joshua 20:7–8 the cities are listed: Kedesh, Shechem, Kiriath Arba (Hebron), Bezer, Ramoth, and Golan.

R

regeneration   Attainment of new spiritual life by the Holy Spirit that naturally leads to moral renewal and transformation (lit., "rebirth"). The term, with this meaning, appears only in Titus 3:5, but the concept is prevalent throughout the New Testament (see John 3:3–5; Rom. 6:1–11; 2 Cor. 5:17; 1 Peter 1:3). In Matthew 19:28 regeneration refers to the future RESURRECTION and cosmic renewal. See also BORN AGAIN.

regula fidei   Lat., "rule of faith." The term refers to that which guides believers and provides criteria for defining the Christian tradition and ORTHODOXY. In the early church, the expansion of the apostolic message (the kerygma) or the BAPTISMAL FORMULA in the formation of creeds and confessions; during the REFORMA-TION, the Bible itself.

reign of Christ See MILLENNIUM, THE.

relative Shorthand for a RELATIVE PRONOUN, adjective, adverb, or clause.

relative clause A CLAUSE introduced by a RELATIVE PRONOUN (e.g., "who," "which"), which contains additional information about the person or thing to which it refers.

relative pronoun A PRONOUN that introduces a RELATIVE CLAUSE, referring to a NOUN in another clause.

religio-historical criticism The comparative study of the religions of the ancient Near East. It is also called the history of religions or comparative religions.

Religionsgeschichte German, "History of religion."

remnant A portion of a group that remains faithful to God after others have fallen away. For example, during Elijah's ministry, BAAL worship predominated, but a remnant continued to serve YAHWEH (1 Kings 19:18; see also Rom. 11:4). Also a remnant of Jews returned to Israel after the BABYLONIAN CAPTIVITY.

repentance Biblical term (based on several Hebrew and Greek words) generally denoting a change in the moral direction of one's life or the repudiation of sinful practices (Job 42:6; Ps. 7:12; Jer. 15:7; 26:3; Acts 17:30; Rev. 9:20). Some translations speak of God's "repenting" in the sense that he changed his course of action or "changed his mind" (Ex. 32:14; Num. 23:19). The theme of repentance was a major component of John the Baptist's mission (Matt. 3:8, 11; Mark 1:4; Luke 3:3), as well as the preaching of Jesus (Matt. 3:2; Mark 1:15; Luke 5:32) and the early church (Acts 2:38; 3:19; 8:22; 26:20). See also METANOIA.

replacement theme A recurrent theme in John's gospel, whereby Jesus is presented as the substitute for various Jewish institutions, such as the major feasts (John 1:29, 36; 7:38–39; 8:12; 9:5), the temple (2:21), and so on.

replacement theology The view that the church replaces ISRAEL in God's plan of SALVATION. Often associated with DISPENSATIONALISM.

reprobation God's passing over some persons (the nonelect), leaving them in their sinful state so that they are condemned to eternal punishment. In DOUBLE PRESDESTINATION, God's choice to condemn some persons to eternal punishment.

resident alien A person who lives in a country but is not a citizen. Some translations use the word "sojourner." According to MOSAIC LAW, resident aliens in Israel were to be afforded fair treatment (Ex. 22:21; Lev. 19:34; Deut. 10:19). See also ALIEN.

resistible grace See IRRESISTIBLE GRACE.

restitution theory See GAP THEORY.

restoration of Israel The view that prior to the end of the world the Jewish people, according to biblical prophecy, will acknowledge Jesus as the MESSIAH and experience God's blessings in the land of PALESTINE (Rom. 11:11–32). See also Gen. 15:18–21; Amos 9:14–15.

resurrection Returning to life. The Old Testament says little about resurrection, although a few people were restored to life

(1 Kings 17:17–24; 2 Kings 4:18–37; 13:21) and a few passages speak about it (Ps. 49:14–15; Ezek. 37:3–14; Dan. 12:2). In the New Testament Jesus raises people from the dead (Luke 8:49–55; John 11:43–44) and predicts his own resurrection (e.g., Matt. 16:21; Mark 8:31; Luke 9:22). For believers, Christ's resurrection is paradigmatic; since he was raised, there is assurance of the same for his followers (1 Cor. 6:14; 15:20; 2 Cor. 4:14).

retribution theology   A belief system holding the view that God punishes people for their wrong actions. The term is frequently used with reference to Deuteronomic THEOLOGY and WISDOM LITERATURE because this concept is pervasive (see DEUTERONOMISTIC HISTORY).

return of Christ   See SECOND COMING.

revealer myth   A second-century Gnostic teaching about a divine messenger who visits earth to reveal to humankind that they have a "divine spark" within them. Discovering this, Gnostics believed, was SALVATION. See also GNOSTICISM.

revelation   In THEOLOGY, disclosure of God's nature or purposes, either through creation (GENERAL REVELATION) or the Scriptures or Christ himself (SPECIAL REVELATION).

revelation, general   See GENERAL REVELATION.

revelation, special   See SPECIAL REVELATION.

rhetoric   The craft of effective communication, including argumentation (i.e., building a case) and the art of persuasion.

rhetorical criticism   A method of studying the biblical text, especially Paul's letters, from the perspective of classical RHETORIC.

rhetorical question A statement that resembles a question but does not call for a response (see Mark 3:23: "How can Satan drive out Satan?").

rib A literary form that resembles a lawsuit, which usually contains several parts: a call to order or a summons to the offending party, a statement of the complaint or accusation, the defendant's response, an appeal to witnesses, and an indictment (see Mic. 6:1–16).

righteousness A term used broadly in the Bible of a state of moral purity in ethical matters or right living (Gen. 18:23; likewise of God, Ps. 7:11; Isa. 5:16), especially a lifestyle in accordance with God's law (Pss. 15:2; 37:21). In THEOLOGY, the term refers to the righteous state in which Adam and Eve lived prior to the FALL (i.e., ORIGINAL RIGHTEOUSNESS); the guiltless life and perfect obedience of the Son of God (i.e., Christ's righteousness; 1 John 2:1); the crediting of Christ's moral perfection to believers (i.e., imputed righteousness; Rom. 4:3–5; see IMPUTATION); and the progressive change in character that believers experience by the power of the Holy Spirit (Eph. 5:9).

rigorous eclecticism In TEXTUAL CRITICISM, an approach to deciding between variants that relies almost exclusively on INTERNAL EVIDENCE—evidence pertaining to a biblical author's vocabulary, style, and so on (also called intrinsic evidence) and the habits of SCRIBES (often termed transcriptional probabilities).

R

ritual acts Prescribed actions, usually as part of a religious ceremony or rite, for such purposes as appeasing a DEITY, attaining ritual purity, and so on.

ritual decalogue A set of cultic laws in Exodus 34, believed by some to be a primitive decalogue.

Roman Catholicism See CATHOLICISM.

Roman period   Period of time approximating the dominance of Rome in the ancient world, from the fifth century B.C.E. to the fifth century C.E.

root   The basic or minimal form of a word, without declensional endings and with all the affixes removed. Root words in Hebrew ordinarily appear as three consonants (called RADICALS or root letters).

Rosh Hashanah   In JUDAISM, New Year, celebrated on the first day of the month of Tishri (corresponding to our September/October). See also FEAST OF TRUMPETS.

Rosh Hodesh   The new moon Festival (Heb., "beginning of a lunar month").

rough breathing   In Greek, the small symbol that stands above vowels at the beginning of some words, indicating that they should be pronounced with an "h" sound.

royal grant covenant   See COVENANT OF GRANT.

royal plural   The practice of a king or queen to use first person plural pronouns ("we," "our," "us," etc.) instead of the singular when speaking officially. Some understand the Old Testament passages in which God uses plural pronouns for himself as the royal plural (e.g., Gen. 1:26).

ruin-reconstruction theory   See GAP THEORY.

R

S

Sabbath   According to the Jewish calendar, the seventh day of the week, set aside for worship and rest (Heb., *shabbat*, "rest"). Jews observe the Sabbath as a holy day (see Ex. 20:8; Deut. 5:14); Christians, on the other hand, generally set aside Sunday, the first day of the week, as the special day of worship, though they may refer to it as the Sabbath.

Sabellianism   The view of Sabellius (early third century), who taught that God revealed himself successively in three modes: first as the Father who created the COSMOS and gave the MOSAIC LAW to Israel; secondly as the Son, the Redeemer; finally as the Spirit, who imparts grace. Thus in Sabellianism there is only one divine Person; the TRINITY is denied. See also MODALISM, MONARCHIANISM, PATRIPASSIANISM.

sacral kingship   A view of kingship in which it is thought that kings are mediators between God and their people.

sacrament   An outward action or sign that according to Protestant tradition encourages or validates faith, or which according to Roman Catholic tradition, effects or conveys grace. While the majority of Protestants recognize two sacraments—BAPTISM and COMMUNION (some include FOOTWASHING)—Roman Catholics recognize seven.

sacred history   See SALVATION HISTORY.

sacrifice Something offered to God, especially an animal, as an act of worship or for obtaining forgiveness (Ex. 20:24; Lev. 1–7). In the New Testament, believers are not required to offer animal sacrifices according to the MOSAIC COVENANT because Jesus Christ gave his life as the ultimate sacrifice for sin (Heb. 10:12). However, Christians are called to offer themselves as "living sacrifices" (Rom. 12:1; see also 1 Peter 2:5).

Sadducees A group drawn mainly from the priestly aristocracy in JUDAISM from the second century B.C.E. to the first century C.E., who evidently were skeptical of Pharisaic traditions and teachings, especially about the RESURRECTION, angels, and fate versus FREE WILL. Yet both the origin of the group and precisely what they believed is obscured by the fact that extant sources are all prejudiced against them. In the Synoptic Gospels the PHARISEES and Sadducees are hostile to Jesus (Matt. 16:1; Mark 12:18).

saga A common narrative GENRE that depicts events vividly and contains fundamental truths apart from historical consideration. The story of Sodom in Genesis 19 is classified as a saga.

salvation In THEOLOGY, God's gracious work of rescuing people from SIN and bringing them into a right relationship with himself (Acts 4:12). The term encompasses several other key doctrines: JUSTIFICATION, in which believers are declared innocent; SANCTIFICATION, in which believers are progressively "saved" from the power of sin; and GLORIFICATION, in which believers are finally saved from judgment and the domination of evil. The term is sometimes used synonymously with justification.

salvation history A perspective on history that highlights the divine plan, especially God's redemptive purposes and the broad theme of promise–fulfillment. Also called sacred history or referred to by the German term *HEILSGESCHICHTE*.

Samaritan Pentateuch   An edition of the PENTATEUCH written in archaic Hebrew script, preserved in the Samaritan community during the Second Temple period, and allied with the Palestinian text family.

Samaritans   A small Jewish religious sect, whose origin is unclear and who worshiped the God of Israel at Mount Gerizim in Samaria rather than at Jerusalem. The New Testament depicts a situation in which there is hostility between Jews and Samaritans (Luke 10:29–37; 17:11–19; John 4:9).

sanctification   Making something or someone clean or holy. In THEOLOGY, sanctification refers to God's work of transforming believers so that the legal declaration of innocence (JUSTIFICATION) is progressively worked out in life experience through the power of the Holy Spirit (Rom. 6:19; Phil. 1:6; 1 Thess. 4:3).

sanctuary   A place of worship, such as Israel's TABERNACLE or TEMPLE (Ex. 25:8).

Sanhedrin   Term used in the MISHNAH and in the New Testament of courts generally (Matt. 5:22; 10:17; Mark 13:9) and of Jerusalem's highest tribunal, a council presided over by the HIGH PRIEST (Matt. 26:59; Mark 14:55; Acts 5:21).

sapiential   Of or relating to wisdom or to the Wisdom books of the Old Testament (Lat., *sapientia,* "wisdom"). Sometimes the term includes texts outside the Old Testament, including portions of the New Testament.

Sarai   Wife of Abram/Abraham before God changed her name to Sarah (Gen. 17:15).

Satan   Throughout the Hebrew Bible the term is used of adversaries and accusers generally (Heb. for "adversary"; see Num. 22:22,

32; 1 Kings 11:14, 23, 25; Ps. 109:4, 6). In some of the Old Testament books, it refers to a particular ANGEL in Yahweh's heavenly court who indicts sinners (Job 1:6–2:7; Zech. 3:1–2). In intertestamental Jewish writings, extending into the New Testament, the term is used as a proper name for a supernatural being who stands in opposition to God and God's people (Matt. 12:26; 16:23; Luke 22:31; 2 Cor. 12:7; Rev. 12:9; 20:2, 7). See also DEVIL.

satisfaction theory of the atonement The view normally associated with Anselm (1033–1109) that Jesus died to satisfy God's just demands; that is, Christ's redemptive work in ATONEMENT was not primarily directed at humanity (e.g., an example of God's love) but rather at God the Father. Also referred to as the commercial theory of the atonement and the PENAL-SUBSTITUTION THEORY OF THE ATONEMENT.

satrap Title of provincial rulers in the Persian Empire (see Ezra 8:36; Est. 3:12; 9:3; Dan. 3:2–3; 6:1–7).

savior Generally, one who saves or rescues, whether from imminent danger (2 Sam. 22:3; Isa. 43:11; see also Ps. 106:21) or from spiritual death (Luke 1:47). In the New Testament, the term is reserved almost exclusively for Jesus (Luke 2:11; Acts 5:31; Phil. 3:20; 1 Tim. 1:1; Titus 3:6). See also SALVATION.

sayings source A source, containing mostly Jesus' sayings, that many scholars believe was used independently by Matthew and Luke in composing their Gospels. Usually referred to as Q (see also Q).

scribal error An obvious mistake made by a scribe in the copying of a document.

scribal gloss Additions to a text made by a scribe while copying the text, either for the purpose of clarification or for correction. Same as GLOSS.

scribes   People trained in reading and writing so as to be employed as clerks, secretaries, and archivists, handling business, legal, financial, and government records (2 Sam. 8:17; 2 Kings 12:10; 18:18; 22:3, 12; Jer. 32:12; 36:10). The term eventually referred more specifically to those who transmitted and interpreted Jewish law (Ezra 7:6, 10). By the first century, Jewish scribes served as "teachers of the law," providing religious interpretations of the customary laws in the Old Testament (Matt. 5:20; 8:19; 23:2; Mark 2:15–17; 7:1–8). The New Testament suggests that, at the grassroots level, many Jews did not consider their interpretations authoritative.

scriptio continua   Latin term for writing without any spaces between words and sentences; a characteristic of Greek manuscripts, but not of Hebrew.

scriptio defectiva   Latin, "defective writing."

Scriptures   Designation for the biblical writings, the Bible.

scroll   A document of leather or PAPYRUS that is rolled up.

Sea of Reeds   Body of water mentioned in the Bible (Heb., *Yam Suph*), particularly in the Exodus narrative (Ex. 13:18; 15:4, 22). In the Septuagint the term was rendered "Red Sea."

Sea Peoples   A group of peoples from throughout the Mediterranean whose attacks on ancient civilizations are recorded in Egyptian literature.

Second Advent   See ADVENT; SECOND COMING.

Second Coming   The return of Jesus Christ to earth (Matt. 24:26–44; 26:64; Mark 13:26; Luke 21:27; John 14:3; Acts 3:19–21; 2 Thess. 1:7, 10; Titus 2:13; 1 John 2:28). Some groups, particularly PRETRIBULATIONISM, hold to the IMMINENCE of the Second Coming—that is, it could happen at any time, though it will occur in two stages (see RAPTURE). Also called the Second ADVENT. See also ESCHATOLOGY.

Second Isaiah See DEUTERO-ISAIAH.

second person of the Trinity Designation for JESUS CHRIST. See also TRINITY.

second resurrection A concept that some derive from Revelation 20:5–6, according to which some people are not raised until the end of the MILLENNIUM. Premillennialists understand this as a RESURRECTION of unbelievers only.

Second Temple period The period of time from the rebuilding of the Jerusalem TEMPLE (c. 515 B.C.E.) until 70 C.E., when it was destroyed.

Second Zechariah The latter portion of the book of Zechariah (chs. 9–14), believed by some to date from the Greek period.

seer One who "sees" into (i.e., experiences or interprets) visions and/or dreams (2 Chron. 9:29; Amos 7:12). The term can be used synonymously with "prophet" (1 Sam. 9:9).

selah A transliterated Hebrew word that appears frequently in the book of Psalms, a cue for the worshipers to pause or to reflect, or a musical notation of some other sort.

Seleucids Dynasty founded by Seleucus Nicator (c. 358–281 B.C.E.), one of Alexander the Great's generals; this dynasty ruled over Syria-Palestine from 311 to 64 B.C.E., when they were conquered by Rome.

semantics   The study of meaning in language.

Semite   According to the Old Testament, a descendant of Noah's eldest son, Shem (Gen. 10), who is the ancestor of the Israelites and whose progeny is associated with peoples who would later reside to the east of Israel (e.g., the Arameans, Assyrians, Babylonians, and Persians).

Semitic   Of or pertaining to the race, culture, or language of the Semites. SEMITIC LANGUAGES include AKKADIAN, ARABIC, ARAMAIC, and HEBREW.

Semitic languages   A family of languages in the Near East, subdivided into East Semitic (AKKADIAN), South Semitic (ARABIC and Ethiopic), and West Semitic (such as HEBREW, ARAMAIC, Phoenician, and UGARITIC).

Semitism   Any characteristic of the SEMITIC languages—particularly HEBREW and ARAMAIC—that is carried over into the Greek style of the New Testament or the SEPTUAGINT. Semitisms encompass HEBRAISMS and ARAMAISMS specifically.

sensus plenior   The "fuller sense" (from Latin) of a biblical text, which was not intended by the original author, but which may come to light later, especially with later REVELATION. *Sensus plenior* usually arises in discussion of how the New Testament writers used Old Testament texts.

Septuagint   The Greek TRANSLATION of the Old Testament produced around 200 B.C.E., according to tradition, by seventy translators (Lat., *septuaginta*, "seventy"). The Septuagint became very popular; in the New Testament it is cited more frequently than the original Hebrew. Abbreviated LXX.

sepulcher   A tomb.

S

Sermon on the Mount The conventional name given to the ethical teachings of Jesus presented in Matthew 5–7. The Sermon on the Mount begins with the Beatitudes.

Sermon on the Plain Luke's equivalent to Matthew's SERMON ON THE MOUNT.

servant of Yahweh See SUFFERING SERVANT.

Servant Songs Designation for Isaiah 42:1–4; 49:1–6; 50:4–9; 52:13–53:12 because these passages describe one who is a servant of the Lord. See also SUFFERING SERVANT.

seven deadly sins According to tradition, seven offenses that were thought particularly appalling in the early church: pride, greed, lust, envy, gluttony, anger, and sloth.

seven last words of Christ Designation for the seven statements, if the Gospel accounts are harmonized, spoken by Jesus while on the cross.

seven signs of Christ Designation for the seven miracles (i.e., signs) that Jesus performed in the gospel of John: changing water to wine (2:1–11); healing the official's son (4:46–54); healing by the pool of Bethesda (5:1–9); feeding the 5,000 (6:5–13); walking on water (6:19–21); healing the man born blind (9:1–7); and raising Lazarus from the dead (11:1–44).

S

Shalem A god attested in second-millennium-B.C.E. UGARITIC texts, whom some have suggested served as patron DEITY of the city of Jerusalem during the BRONZE AGE. The name occurs in first-millennium-B.C.E. personal names. It has been suggested that the name of Solomon, king of Jerusalem, invokes this god, though traditionally his name has been construed as derivative of *shalom*, "Peace."

shalom   HEBREW, "peace, wholeness, completeness, harmony." The word is used numerous times in the Old Testament, conveying ideas such as the absence of strife, harmony between people or between nations, an individual's welfare, and the fulfillment that comes from God's presence and BLESSING. Also used as a greeting and in blessings.

Shammaites   A school within the sect of the PHARISEES that followed the more conservative legal interpretations of Rabbi Shammai (late first century B.C.E.).

shavuot   Hebrew, "weeks." See FEAST OF WEEKS.

Shekinah   The radiance or presence of God, or God himself. The term does not appear in the Old Testament but originated in the Jewish tradition of biblical interpretation and refers to a divine manifestation or to God's dwelling (literally, the term is Heb. for "dwelling"). It is often used synonymously with "GLORY" (sometimes referred to as the "Shekinah glory").

Shema   Hebrew, "hear." From the opening word of Deuteronomy 6:4, it refers to the affirmation recited in SYNAGOGUE services: "Hear, O Israel: The LORD our God, the LORD is one."

Sheol   The Hebrew name for the underworld, the place of the dead. See also HADES.

Shephelah   The geographical region between the coastal plain of Philistia to the west and the hills of southern JUDAH to the east. A number of battles described in the Bible took place in the Shephelah (see Josh. 10; Judg. 13–16; 2 Chron. 11:5–12).

shewbread   See BREAD OF THE PRESENCE.

Shiloh   An ancient Israelite village in central PALESTINE where a SANCTUARY to YAHWEH was located during the PREMONARCHIC

PERIOD. To refute the popular belief that Yahweh would never allow Jerusalem to be destroyed because the TEMPLE was located there, Jeremiah recalled that centuries earlier Yahweh had permitted Shiloh to be destroyed even though a Yahwist sanctuary had been located there (Jer. 7:12–14).

shofar A ram's horn, used as a trumpet, which was sounded during the holy days beginning prior to New Year (see ROSH HASHANAH) until the end of YOM KIPPUR.

shorter reading In TEXTUAL CRITICISM, a variation of a text that has fewer words or characters than another manuscript READING for the same passage. Shorter readings are often ORIGINAL, because scribes tended to add rather than delete material.

showbread See BREAD OF THE PRESENCE.

Sicarii A group of Jewish revolutionaries around the time of Christ who often murdered fellow Jews who did not support their more radical religious and political agenda.

sigla Plural of SIGLUM.

siglum An abbreviation or symbol.

sign gifts Term used to denote a group of spiritual gifts that are thought to be "signs" (see 1 Cor. 14:22), indicating God's special presence or serving to confirm the preaching of the GOSPEL, and so on. The term usually refers to the gifts of miracles, healing, prophecy, and SPEAKING IN TONGUES.

signet A device that makes an impression, especially to authenticate a document; a stamp or seal. Used especially of rings (i.e., "signet ring"; Gen. 41:42; Est. 3:10, 12; Isa. 3:21).

signs source   A hypothetical document that many scholars believe was used as a source for John's Gospel, providing a narrative of some of Jesus' miracles.

Simchat Torah   A Hebrew term meaning "rejoicing in Torah." An annual celebration during the FEAST OF TABERNACLES at which the reading of the TORAH is finished and also recommenced with Genesis 1.

simile   A figure of speech containing an explicitly stated comparison, as in "I laid a foundation as an expert builder" (1 Cor. 3:10; see also 1 Peter 1:24). See also METAPHOR.

simony   The buying or selling of church offices; or more generally, any kind of religious work that is essentially mercenary or involves buying or selling spiritual things. The term is derived from the story of Simon Magus in Acts 8:18–24.

sin   General term for any action that constitutes breaking God's MORAL LAW or failure to live up to one's responsibilities before God (Ex. 32:33; Ps. 51:4; Rom. 6:23).

sin offering   A special type of offering that had the effect of purifying the sanctuary from ceremonial contamination (Lev. 4:1–5:13; Num. 15:22–31) so that Yahweh would continue to accept worshipers and their sacrifices.

Sinaiticus   See CODEX SINAITICUS.

sinlessness   The state or condition of being without SIN.

sinlessness of Christ   The view that Jesus Christ was without SIN, a doctrine asserted in several biblical passages (2 Cor. 5:21; Heb. 4:15; 1 John 3:5) and affirmed by the Council of Chalcedon (451 C.E.).

S

sins of commission Sins that involve conduct—they are carried out by actions—in contrast to SINS OF OMISSION.

sins of ignorance Sins committed in ignorance of God's law.

sins of omission Sins that are counted against a person because of failure to act, in contrast to SINS OF COMMISSION.

Sitz im Leben German, "setting in life." This term refers to the original cultural context or church situation from which a certain literary form or passage arose.

Sitz im Leben Jesu German, "setting in the life of Jesus."

Sitz im Leben Kirche German, "setting in the life of the church."

sojourner See RESIDENT ALIEN.

sola fide A slogan and rallying cry of the Protestant REFORMATION affirming that JUSTIFICATION is by faith alone (Lat., "faith alone") rather than by human merit or good works.

sola gratia A slogan and rallying cry of the Protestant REFORMATION affirming that God initiates and accomplishes SALVATION, so that it is entirely an act of grace (Lat., "grace alone") and not based on human accomplishment.

sola Scriptura A slogan and rallying cry of the Protestant REFORMATION affirming that believers are to depend entirely on the Bible (Lat., "Scripture alone") for the message of SALVATION and for the church's authority, as opposed to ecclesiastical tradition or papal authority (see also PAPACY).

Solomon's temple The TEMPLE structure built in Jerusalem under the supervision of King Solomon in the tenth century B.C.E.

(see 1 Kings 5:13–8:66; 2 Chron. 3–4). It was destroyed in 587/586 B.C.E. during the Babylonian invasion (2 Kings 25:9; 2 Chron. 36:19).

Son of Man   Jesus' most frequently used designation for himself (Matt. 9:6; Mark 10:45), which, based on Old Testament usage, can either refer to humankind (Ezek. 2:1) or to an apocalyptic figure who will judge humanity (Dan. 7:13–14).

sopher   Hebrew for "scribe." The term refers to teachers and copyists of the Hebrew Bible. Plural, "*sopherim*."

sopherim   Hebrew for "scribes, bookmen." See SOPHER.

soteriology   Theological study of SALVATION, including theories of the atonement, the doctrines of election and eternal security, and the nature of the gospel.

soul   The immaterial part of a person (Mark 8:36–37), especially the emotional center, the "heart" (see Ps. 63:1; Song 1:7; Matt. 26:38). Sometimes the term is used synonymously with SPIRIT.

soul sleep   According to some theologians, an unconscious state that people experience between death and the final RESURRECTION (see 1 Cor. 15:20; 1 Thess. 4:13–15; 5:10; 2 Peter 3:4).

source criticism   The discipline that attempts to discover and analyze the sources behind a literary work or part of a work. In biblical studies, source critical questions usually center around the PENTATEUCH (the first five books of the Hebrew Bible) and the SYNOPTIC GOSPELS (Matthew, Mark, and Luke), the authors of which evidently used sources.

southern kingdom   The name given to the tribes of JUDAH and Benjamin in the south of ISRAEL, which comprised one nation

S

after the division of the twelve tribes in 931 B.C.E. Also known simply as Judah. See also DIVIDED KINGDOM and NORTHERN KINGDOM.

sovereignty of God God's absolute authority over and management of humankind and the universe (see Isa. 45:5–6; Rom. 9:20–21).

speaking in tongues The miraculous vocalization of words in a language unknown to the speaker. Luke describes a scene on the day of PENTECOST in which believers spoke in tongues under the influence of the Holy Spirit (Acts 2:1–13), as well as subsequent occurrences involving the same phenomenon (10:46; 19:6). Paul uses the same terminology to describe a gift of the Holy Spirit that the Corinthian congregation had experienced (1 Cor. 12:10, 28, 30; 14:2–4), although some view this as a different phenomenon, possibly a heavenly language (cf. 13:1).

special calling See EFFECTUAL CALLING.

special revelation Disclosure of things, especially God's nature, that cannot be known generally through nature or through a person's natural reasoning powers (i.e., GENERAL REVELATION), but only in the Scriptures and through the person of Christ.

spirit Generally, a noncorporeal being. In the Bible this frequently refers to angels or demons ("evil spirits"; 1 Sam. 16:14; Mark 9:25), as well as to the third person of the TRINITY, the Holy Spirit of God (Ezek. 3:14, 24; Luke 4:14; Rom. 8:5; 1 Thess. 5:19). The term is also used of the human SOUL (Isa. 54:6; Matt. 5:3).

spiritual gifts Abilities given by the Holy Spirit to believers for the edification of the church (Rom. 14:19; 15:2; 1 Cor. 12:7; 13:1–3; 14:12, 26; Eph. 4:12, 16; 1 Peter 4:10), as well as for authenticating God's revelation (i.e., "signs"; Acts 14:3;

Rom. 15:19). The New Testament contains several lists of spiritual gifts—none of them alike and none of them exhaustive: Romans 12:6–8; 1 Corinthians 12:8–10; Ephesians 4:11; 1 Peter 4:10–11.

spiritual warfare   General term for struggles described in portions of the Bible, in which angels and/or demons fight, or in which believers on earth, through their prayers, overcome evil spiritual forces (2 Cor. 10:4; Eph. 6:10–18; Rev. 12:7–9).

spiritus asper   Latin for "rough breathing."

spiritus lenis   Latin for "smooth breathing."

spurious reading   In TEXTUAL CRITICISM, a text as it reads in a particular MANUSCRIPT or manuscripts, which is judged to be inauthentic.

stairlike parallelism   See CLIMACTIC PARALLELISM.

stanza   A unit of poetry, consisting of a group of lines that are usually related by a pattern or theme.

stele   A pillar bearing an inscription. Also spelled stela.

step parallelism   See CLIMACTIC PARALLELISM.

stich   The basic unit of Hebrew poetry (Gk., "row, line").

Stoicism   School of Greek philosophy in which impersonal Reason governs the universe. Stoicism emphasized ethical living, harmony with nature, and suppression of one's emotions, among other things. Some scholars have felt that Stoic thought may lie behind John's LOGOS doctrine or that Paul's vocabulary was influenced by Stoicism.

strong waw See WAW CONSECUTIVE.

structural analysis See STRUCTURALISM.

structural criticism See STRUCTURALISM.

structural exegesis See STRUCTURALISM.

structuralism Study of language (likewise, a method of biblical interpretation) in terms of systems and structures, either the surface structures inherent to communication or the underlying structures (i.e., structures of the mind, structures and systems of the culture, etc.) thought to be coded within texts. Also referred to as structural analysis, exegesis, or criticism, or stylistic criticism.

style In literary studies, a general term for the way something is written. The term refers to a work's distinctive features of expression, such as rhetorical devices, vocabulary, and the use of certain grammatical constructions.

stylistic criticism See STRUCTURALISM.

stylus A pointed instrument for writing or engraving.

subgenre A category of literary composition pertaining to its form, style, and subject matter (see GENRE) that does not affect an entire work.

S

subject The major component in a sentence, normally a noun that functions as the author or agent of the main verbal action.

subjective genitive In Greek, a GENITIVE case word that appears in a construction with its HEAD NOUN; the genitive CASE word functions as the initiator or performer (i.e., the subject) of the verbal notion implied by the head noun. For example, in the phrase, "the love of Christ" (Rom. 8:35), the word "Christ" is in the genitive, functioning in a subjective sense: "Christ's love."

subjunctive mood   In Greek, the MOOD that portrays the verbal action as being possible or probable. In English, "She was browsing the menu, pondering what she *might order* for lunch."

sublapsarianism   The view that God decreed to permit the FALL before decreeing to save the ELECT, in contrast to SUPRALAP-SARIANISM. See also INFRALAPSARIANISM.

subordinate clause   A CLAUSE that is dependent on another clause. Also called a dependent clause. See also SUPERORDINATE CLAUSE.

substantive   A NOUN or another word or group of words that functions like a noun.

substitutionary atonement   See PENAL-SUBSTITUTION THEORY OF THE ATONEMENT.

Suffering Servant   Designation for a person or persons described in Isaiah 52:13–53:12, who suffers for others and then is exalted. Other so-called SERVANT SONGS appear in Isaiah 42:1–4; 49:1–6; 50:4–9. Isaiah identifies the servant as Israel (41:8; 44:1–2, 21; 45:4; 49:3), although early Christians saw in this MOTIF a reference to Jesus Christ (Matt. 8:17; 12:18–21; John 12:38; Acts 8:32–35).

suffix   A language element affixed to the end of a word, changing its meaning in some way.

Sukkot   See FEAST OF TABERNACLES.

summum bonum   Latin for "highest good," referring to God as the source and end of all good.

superlative degree Denoting comparison that speaks of the highest degree, as in the adjective "strictest" in "the strictest sect of our religion" (Acts 26:5). This is in contrast to the COMPARATIVE DEGREE and POSITIVE DEGREE.

superordinate clause The MAIN CLAUSE of a sentence, in contrast to the SUBORDINATE CLAUSE.

superscription A heading that appears before a large number of the Psalms, containing information related to traditional authorship (e.g., Pss. 15; 26; 32; 50; 101), genre (e.g., Pss. 16; 75; 108), directions for reading or singing (e.g., Pss. 12; 55), or situational details pertaining to the origin of the psalm (e.g., Pss. 3; 18; 60).

supralapsarianism The view that God decreed the ELECTION of some and the REPROBATION of others before allowing the FALL, in contrast to SUBLAPSARIANISM. See also DOUBLE PREDESTINATION.

suzerainty treaty See SUZERAIN-VASSAL COVENANT.

suzerain-vassal covenant A treaty or COVENANT issued by a powerful king (suzerain), who promises to protect, and a subordinate or minor king, who promises to obey the laws of the suzerain. This sort of covenant usually includes blessings for treaty loyalty and curses for disloyalty. Examples in the Old Testament are the Sinai covenant and the entire book of Deuteronomy. Contrast COVENANT OF GRANT.

symbolic discourse A GENRE in which a METAPHOR is extended so that it becomes the backdrop for an extended discourse (e.g., the good shepherd discourse of John 10).

Symmachus A Greek VERSION of the Old Testament produced at the close of the second century C.E., which is preserved only in the HEXAPLA, a book of six Old Testament texts in parallel columns. Symmachus, the man for whom this version is named, preferred readability to literalness. Jerome consulted it in preparing the VULGATE. See also ORIGEN.

synagogue A gathering place of Jews for worship, reading of the Scriptures, and religious instruction (Gk., "gathering together"). Many believe the synagogue originated while the Jews were exiled in Babylonia without a TEMPLE. By Jesus' day, synagogues were a common part of Jewish life (Matt. 4:23; Luke 4:15, 44). Likewise Paul visited numerous synagogues as he traveled around regions bordering the Mediterranean Sea (Acts 13:5; 14:1; 15:21; 17:1).

synchronic Pertaining to events or things at a particular time rather than over time. The opposite of DIACHRONIC.

syncretism The fusion of doctrines and practices from dissimilar or opposing religious systems, which results in one new system.

synecdoche A figure of speech in which a part of something refers to the whole or vice versa, as in "Moses" standing for the entire Old Testament (2 Cor. 3:15).

synonymous parallelism A feature of Hebrew poetry in which one line repeats the thought of a preceding line but in different terms (e.g., Isa. 1:3).

synopsis A book that displays the SYNOPTIC GOSPELS—Matthew, Mark, and Luke—in columns in order to show their resemblance (i.e., verbal agreement).

Synoptic Gospels The biblical books of Matthew, Mark, and Luke. They are called "synoptic" because they recount many of the same stories, often with similar (sometimes exact) wording, and in the same order generally, so that their stories can be laid side-by-side and "seen together" ("synoptic" means "seen together"). See also SYNOPTIC PROBLEM.

Synoptic problem   The difficulty of explaining the literary similarities and differences between Matthew, Mark, and Luke (the SYNOPTIC GOSPELS), including not only large sections in which there is exact verbal correspondence, but also the arrangement of material and order of events. This riddle was discovered and discussed early—the church fathers disagreed on the issue. Most scholars today believe that Mark was written first and was used independently by Matthew and Luke (see Luke 1:1–4), who each had access to another source, Q. See also MARKAN PRIORITY/ HYPOTHESIS, MATTHEAN PRIORITY/HYPOTHESIS, and Q.

syntax   The study of words, phrases, clauses, and sentences, especially their arrangement and the rules inherent to forming intelligible communication.

synthetic parallelism   A term sometimes used to describe a feature of Hebrew POETRY, in which two lines discuss the same topic—the second line usually advances the thought of the first (e.g., Prov. 4:23). See also CONTINUOUS PARALLELISM.

Syria   In ancient history, the region east of the Mediterranean, north of PALESTINE, and extending to the Euphrates to the northeast (Matt. 4:24; Luke 2:2; Acts 15:41; Gal. 1:21). A number of Syrian cities are important relative to biblical history: Ebla (see EBLA TABLETS), UGARIT (see RAS SHAMRA TABLETS), and Syrian Antioch ("Antioch" in Acts 13:1).

Syrian text-type   See BYZANTINE TEXT-TYPE.

Syro-Ephraimitic crisis   The political crisis of 734–733 B.C.E. when Syria and Israel (also called Ephraim) attacked

S

Jerusalem. It provides the background for Isaiah's IMMANUEL prophecy (Isa. 7:14).

systematic theology The study of Christian doctrines within their respective classifications, such as ECCLESIOLOGY (the study of the church), PNEUMATOLOGY (the study of the Holy Spirit), and so on. Thus systematic theology begins with a topic and seeks to understand the Bible's comprehensive teachings on that subject. See also THEOLOGY.

S

tabernacle   The movable tent in which the Jewish people worshiped during the period of wandering (Ex. 25–27; 35:10–38:31). Supposedly the Jerusalem TEMPLE was patterned after this tabernacle. The writer of the book of Hebrews says that Christ performed priestly duties in a heavenly tabernacle (Heb. 8:2, 5; 9:11, 21).

Tabernacles, Feast of   See FEAST OF TABERNACLES.

Table of Nations   Designation for the description in Genesis 10 of the expansion of humankind from Noah and his sons to numerous and diverse peoples who dispersed across the ANCIENT NEAR EAST. In the book of Genesis the Table of Nations functions to demonstrate the outworking of the divine mandate that humankind should, "Be fruitful and increase in number; fill the earth and subdue it" (Gen. 1:28; cf. 9:1, 7). It also has strong thematic ties with Genesis 9, particularly Noah's cursing and BLESSING (9:25–27), as well as the story of the tower of Babel in 11:1–9.

Tacitus   A Roman historian of the second century C.E. whose account of first-century Rome is crucial for historians.

tag   A grammatical label attached to a word or other language element (a word's part of speech, CASE, TENSE, relation to other words, etc.), especially in electronic texts so that a sizeable portion

235

of text or an entire work (e.g., the Old Testament, Luke–Acts, etc.) can be searched for certain features, patterns, and so on.

Talmud The MISHNAH (a compilation of rabbinic traditional material) plus the GEMARA (a lengthy written commentary). The PALESTINIAN TALMUD includes the Mishnah plus the Palestinian Gemara; the BABYLONIAN TALMUD includes the Mishnah plus the Babylonian Gemara. The word "Talmud" derives from a Hebrew word meaning "study."

Tanak A term used by Jews to describe the same collection of books that Christians call the "Old Testament." It is an acronym comprised of the initial letters of the Hebrew names for the Old Testament's three basic divisions: TORAH (the PENTATEUCH), NEBIIM (Prophets), and KETUBIM (WRITINGS). Also Tanakh.

Tanna See TANNAIM.

Tannaim Jewish scribes who during the first two centuries C.E. passed on the traditions (Heb., "professional repeater," or "transmitter"). Tannaitic literature includes the MISHNAH and TOSEFTA.

Tannaitic See TANNAIM.

targum ARAMAIC translations of the Hebrew Bible with additional commentary.

taryag Hebrew word whose consonants form the numerical equivalent of 613, which is the number of laws that Jews counted in the TORAH.

Tatian's Harmony See DIATESSARON.

tax collector In the New Testament, someone authorized to collect taxes for the Roman government. Because tax collectors took advantage of a system that was ripe for abuse, their title became synonymous with evil, particularly extortion (Matt. 18:17; Luke 18:9–14; 19:2). Matthew (Levi) is described as a tax collector (Matt. 10:3; Luke 5:27).

Teaching of the Twelve Apostles See *DIDACHE*.

tefillin Containers known as "phylacteries" (see Ex. 13:16; Matt. 23:5), referring to the small containers that hold Scripture passages, which are worn by Jews as an act of religious devotion (sing., *tefillah*). Also *tephillin*.

tel See TELL.

teleological argument An argument for the existence of God based on the apparent orderliness of the universe, which presumably implies a grand DESIGNER who superintends all things with a purpose (from Gk., *telos*, "purpose"). The teleological argument is usually associated with Thomas Aquinas (1225–1274 C.E.). See also CLASSICAL APOLOGETICS.

telic Denoting purpose. This term is used of words and grammatical features whenever they convey the notion of purpose (Gk., *telos*, "end, goal").

tell In archaeology, a hill or mound created by successive settlements in the same location. Tell is Arabic, the equivalent of the Hebrew tel.

T

temple In the Bible, the principal sacred structure built as God's "house" (2 Chron. 3:1; Jer. 26:2)—a place for God's people to meet with YAHWEH. SOLOMON'S TEMPLE (cf. 1 Kings 6–7) was completed in the middle of the tenth century B.C.E., destroyed by the Babylonians in 587/586, rebuilt and rededicated by Zerubbabel in 516/515 (i.e., the Second Temple; cf. Ezra 1; 3–6), restored and expanded during the reign of Herod (i.e., HEROD'S TEMPLE; cf. Matt. 21:14–15; John 2:20; Acts 3:1–11; 21:27–29), beginning in 20 B.C.E., and finally destroyed by the Romans in 70 C.E.

temptation   Enticement to SIN. The Bible teaches that temptation is not a sin—Jesus himself was tempted (Mark 1:13; Heb. 2:18; 4:15). In the LORD'S PRAYER Christ's disciples are told to pray that they might not enter into temptation (Matt. 6:13).

Ten Commandments   The ten laws given by God to Moses on Mount Sinai (Ex. 20:1–17; repeated with variation in Deut. 5:6–21), providing the essence of MOSAIC LAW and the basis for Israel's continuing relationship with YAHWEH. Also referred to as the Decalogue (Gk., "ten words"; see also Ex. 34:28; Deut. 4:13; 10:4).

ten words   Another designation for the Decalogue, the TEN COMMANDMENTS.

tense   In English grammar, the time of the verbal action indicated by verbal forms. HEBREW and ARAMAIC, the Old Testament languages, do not have tenses as such; time is indicated in context by adverbs and other grammatical features. In GREEK, tense refers to a category for verbs based on their form (i.e., PRESENT TENSE, FUTURE TENSE, AORIST TENSE, IMPERFECT TENSE, PERFECT TENSE, and PLUPERFECT TENSE).

tent of meeting   A tent set up outside of Israel's camp before the TABERNACLE was constructed (Ex. 33:7), which may have been a simplified form of the tabernacle with a similar function. The term appears almost exclusively in Exodus, Leviticus, and Numbers.

tephillin   See TEFILLIN.

teraphim   Household gods or idols that were worshiped by ancient SEMITIC peoples.

testament   The name used for the two parts of the Christian Bible, the Old and New Testaments. In this sense it means roughly "COVENANT."

Testament of Moses   See ASSUMPTION OF MOSES.

Testaments of the Twelve Patriarchs   Collection of documents modeled on Jacob's "last will and testament" in Genesis 49 (i.e., written as if they were some of Israel's great leaders' final wishes). The *Testament of the Twelve*, as it is sometimes called, was influenced by Hellenistic philosophy and contains numerous exhortations and ethical teachings.

testimonium   An Old Testament quotation cited as a PROOF TEXT to prove that Jesus is the MESSIAH. Plural, testimonia.

tetragrammaton   See YHWH.

tetrarch   Provincial ruler in the early Roman Empire, especially one in PALESTINE (Matt. 14:1; Luke 3:1, 19; 9:7; Acts 13:1).

Tetrateuch   The first four books of the PENTATEUCH, Genesis through Numbers.

text-critical   Related to TEXTUAL CRITICISM.

text-type   A category for Greek manuscripts based on their affinity with large numbers of other manuscripts (i.e., verbal similarity). So while all of the existing biblical manuscripts disagree with one another, they can be grouped into families or text-types because there are patterns of divergence. The names—ALEXANDRIAN TEXT-TYPE, BYZANTINE TEXT-TYPE, and WESTERN TEXT-TYPE—were created based on the supposed origin of the manuscripts.

textual apparatus   See CRITICAL APPARATUS.

T

textual criticism The discipline concerned with studying the disparate MANUSCRIPT evidence for a written work, when the ORIGINAL is no longer in existence, in the hope of discerning the original text. Textual criticism includes gathering and organizing manuscript data, evaluating VARIANT readings, seeking to reconstruct the history of the transmission of texts, and attempting to identify original texts with some degree of certainty. Two types of evidence are discussed in textual criticism. EXTERNAL EVIDENCE pertains to the biblical manuscripts and versions themselves: their quantity, date, character, and so on. INTERNAL EVIDENCE pertains to scribal tendencies as well as the author's style, vocabulary, and argument (the latter is termed intrinsic probability). Also referred to as text criticism.

textual problem A TEXT-CRITICAL issue involving conflicting readings from two or more manuscripts of the Bible in which the solution is not obvious.

textual variant See VARIANT.

Textus Receptus Lat., "received text." Abbreviated TR. See RECEIVED TEXT.

theism Belief in a divine being (i.e., MONOTHEISM) or beings (e.g., TRITHEISM, POLYTHEISM).

theistic evolution A mediating view of origins that hypothesizes that a divine creator superintended the world and the cosmos using evolutionary processes.

theocentric God-centered.

theocracy An earthly government that is ruled by God and in which divine law becomes state law. The Old Testament describes Israel in terms of theocratic rule.

theodicy   A vindication of God's goodness and justice in the face of evil and suffering in the world. The book of Job is frequently understood in terms of theodicy.

Theodotion   A Greek VERSION of the Old Testament that is more literal than the SEPTUAGINT in its rendering of the original Hebrew. This text was used by many of the church fathers in the third and fourth centuries. It is named after a man who may have been a proselyte Jew living in the last half of the second century C.E.

theology   Literally, the study of God. The term, however, has broad application—it can refer to the Bible's teaching about God or other related subjects or to a system formulated to express a perspective on the divine purpose and the whole of the Bible's teaching (see also SYSTEMATIC THEOLOGY). Terms such as "JOHANNINE theology" or "PAULINE theology" reflect attempts to derive the distinctive features and emphases from certain portions of the Bible, as compared to BIBLICAL THEOLOGY, which encompasses all of Scripture. Terms such as FEMINIST THEOLOGY and BLACK THEOLOGY indicate an approach to theological exploration from a definitive standpoint. Sometimes the term is used broadly of any synthetic expression of a topic from a biblical perspective (e.g., a theology of church; a theology of material possessions).

theology proper   The study of God, especially the nature of God as TRINITY, the divine attributes, and so on.

theopassianism   See PATRIPASSIANISM.

theophany   A manifestation of God (Gk., "appearance of god"). See also EPIPHANY.

Theophilus   The person to whom Luke's Gospel and the book of Acts were addressed (Luke 1:3; Acts 1:1). The name means

T

"lover or friend of God," leading some to think that it may have been a general designation for the reader rather than a specific individual. However, the honorific title "most excellent" (Luke 1:3) has led others to think that Theophilus was a real person, perhaps a Roman provincial governor or Luke's literary patron.

theophoric   A word, especially a personal name, that refers to a DEITY.

theopneustos   Transliteration of a Greek term that appears in 2 Timothy 3:16 in which "all Scripture"—here referring to the Old Testament—is described as "inspired by God" (lit., "God-breathed"). See also INSPIRATION.

Theotokos   Literally, "God bearer." Early church fathers used the term of Mary, the mother of Jesus, to express the fact that she gave birth to God the Son.

theriolatry   The worship of animals, common in biblical times, but consistently condemned in JUDAISM and Christianity (see Ezek. 8:9–11; Rom. 1:23).

Third Isaiah   See TRITO-ISAIAH.

third person of the Trinity   Designation for the HOLY SPIRIT. See also TRINITY.

Thummim   See URIM AND THUMMIM.

Tiamat   In the ancient Babylonian epic of creation, the *ENUMA ELISH*, the personification of the primeval salt waters.

tiqqune sopherim   In TEXTUAL CRITICISM, a Hebrew term meaning scribal EMENDATION. The *tiqqune sopherim* changes one letter in a word (usually a pronoun, occasionally an entire word) to avoid a reading that was thought to be offensive to God (e.g., "your [God's] ruin" to "my [Moses'] ruin," in Num. 11:15).

tithe A tenth. According to MOSAIC LAW, Israelites were required to give one-tenth of their herds and their crops to support the LEVITICAL PRIESTHOOD (Num. 18:21–24; Deut. 14:22–29).

tittle A small diacritical mark or stroke, such as an accent. The term appears in some translations of Matthew 5:18 (= Luke 16:17), in which Jesus said not one "jot or tittle" of the law would pass away "until all is accomplished." This translates two Greek terms, *iota* and *keraia,* the latter referring to the "hook" or "horn" of some letters that distinguishes them from others.

titulus Designation for the sign (Lat., "title") that Pilate placed on the cross above Jesus, which read "Jesus of Nazareth, the King of the Jews" in Aramaic, Latin, and Greek (John 19:19–20; see also Matt. 27:37; Mark 15:26; Luke 23:38). See also I.N.R.I.

toledot The ten generations (Heb., "generations") of Genesis (see 2:4; 5:1; 6:9; 10:1; 11:10, 27; 25:12, 19; 36:1, 9; 37:2), used to structure the material in that book. Also toledoth.

tongues, gift of See SPEAKING IN TONGUES.

Torah The first five books of the Hebrew Bible; "the law of Moses." Or more generally of divine law or any expression of God's will (Heb., "instruction"). See also LAW.

Tosefta A collection of tannaitic traditions from the third to the fifth centuries C.E., arranged into six main divisions similar to the MISHNAH, but more HAGGADIC in nature and four times longer. See also TANNAIM.

T

total depravity   The first of the five points of CALVINISM (the "T" in TULIP), referring to the pervasive character of humankind's sinful, fallen state, and the inability of people, apart from Christ, to please God or earn his favor. See also CALVINISM, FIVE POINTS OF.

tractate   A treatise or essay; a book or section of the MISHNAH or TALMUD.

traditio-historical criticism   English translation of the German *Traditionsgeschichte.* See TRADITION CRITICISM.

tradition criticism   The scholarly discipline concerned with tracing the history of a tradition over the course of its development. In Old Testament studies, one might trace the development of the Sinai tradition, the David tradition, and so on, in the Old Testament. In New Testament studies, one might trace the period of time between the historical occurrence of the events described in the Gospels and their being recorded in their final form. See also FORM CRITICISM.

traducianism   The view that individual human souls are propagated by parents, as opposed to CREATIONISM, which asserts that God creates each new SOUL at conception. Also called generationism.

transcendence   The quality or state of being outside of or beyond a certain boundary (e.g., the universe, human comprehension). In THEOLOGY, the nature of God as distinct from and in some sense outside of his creation; his "otherness" (Rom. 9:5). Usually held in tension with the notion of God's IMMANENCE, his being near and involved in the world.

transcribe   To make an exact copy of a text.

transcriptional evidence   In TEXTUAL CRITICISM, evidence brought forward for a particular text-critical issue pertaining to the practices and habits of scribes and editors.

transcriptional probability   In TEXTUAL CRITICISM, the likelihood of a scribe doing one thing over another, which provides a basis for choosing among competing textual VARIANTS. In short, scribes tended to smooth out difficult wording, to fill out short passages, and to make explicit anything vague.

Trans-Euphrates   The land to the east of the Euphrates River.

transfiguration   The manifestation of Christ's GLORY, which evidently occurred once during his earthly life (Matt. 17:1–8; Mark 9:2–8; Luke 9:28–36).

transhumance pastoralism   The migration of herdsmen with their livestock with the changing of the seasons.

transitive verb   A VERB that requires a DIRECT OBJECT to complete its meaning. See also INTRANSITIVE VERB.

Transjordan   The plateau east of the Jordan River Valley that borders the great Arabian Desert.

translation   The process or result of rendering something in another language. The term is also used of persons who bypass death and pass immediately into HEAVEN (e.g., Enoch in Gen. 5:24; Heb. 11:5; Elijah in 2 Kings 2:11).

transliteration   A word that has been phonetically rendered in another language by supplying the corresponding letters of the alphabet rather than by translating the meaning of the word. For

T

example, the word "BAPTISM" is a transliterated form of the Greek term *baptizo*, meaning "immerse" or "dip."

transmission   In TEXTUAL CRITICISM, the handing down of the biblical text through history by means of copying and distributing.

transposition   In TEXTUAL CRITICISM, a SCRIBAL ERROR involving a change in the order of letters or words.

transubstantiation   According to Roman Catholic THEOL-OGY, the changing of the eucharistic bread and wine, at the consecration in the Mass, into the actual substance of Jesus' body and blood. See also CONSUBSTANTIATION.

Tree of Life   In the biblical story of Adam and Eve, a tree in the Garden of Eden that presumably would have bestowed immortality to the couple had they not been expelled from the GARDEN OF EDEN (3:22–24). The writer of the book of Revelation uses this tree as a symbol of eternal life (2:7; 22:2, 14, 19). See also TREE OF THE KNOWLEDGE OF GOOD AND EVIL.

Tree of the Knowledge of Good and Evil   In the biblical story of Adam and Eve, a tree in the GARDEN OF EDEN from which the couple was forbidden to eat or else they would die (Gen. 2:16–17). After they did eat from this tree, God increased Eve's pain in childbirth and Adam's pain in working the soil (3:16–19); they were also banished from the garden (vv. 23–24). See also TREE OF LIFE.

tribulation   In general, hardship or suffering, especially affliction for the sake of Christ (Rom. 12:12; 1 Thess. 1:6). Or specifically, the seven-year period preceding the Second Coming (Matt. 24:21). See also MIDTRIBULATIONISM, POSTTRIBULATIONISM, and PRETRIBULATIONISM.

tribulational views   Differing views among fundamentalists (see FUNDAMENTALISM) on eschatological events and the church's relationship to the TRIBULATION period, whether she will be raptured (1 Thess. 4:17) before (i.e., PRETRIBULATIONISM), during (i.e., MIDTRIBULATIONISM), or after (i.e., POSTTRIBULATIONISM) the Tribulation. See also ESCHATOLOGY.

trichotomism   The view that human beings consist of three parts: body, SOUL, and SPIRIT (cf. 1 Thess. 5:23; Heb. 4:12), as opposed to DICHOTOMISM, which only specifies body and soul (cf. Matt. 10:28). See also MONISM.

Trinitarian   Pertaining to the TRINITY.

Trinity   The name for the essential character or nature of God, who exists as three persons—Father, Son, and Holy Spirit—in one GODHEAD. Traditionally, Christians have affirmed three distinct persons who share the same essence or substance.

triple tradition   Material that is common to all three SYNOPTIC GOSPELS: Matthew, Mark, and Luke (approximately 360 verses).

trisagion   The exclamation of praise "Holy, Holy, Holy" (Isa. 6:3; Rev. 4:8; Gk., "thrice holy").

tritheism   Belief in three gods. Some have accused Christians of tritheism since they affirm the existence of three divine persons in the GODHEAD.

Trito-Isaiah   Designation for the "third" part of Isaiah (chs. 56–66), or the supposed author of this literary unit (see also DEUTERO-ISAIAH).

Triumphal Entry   Jesus' entrance into Jerusalem the Sunday before his crucifixion. The crowd that witnessed this event spread articles of clothing and palm branches in Jesus' path (John 12:13; thus the name PALM SUNDAY). This event, attested in all four Gospels (Matt. 21:1–11; Mark 11:1–11; Luke 19:28–44; John 12:12–19), is significant because of the crowd's recognition of Jesus as Messiah and Jesus' acceptance of their praise.

triune   Existing as three in one. The term usually describes God (the triune God), who exists as three persons in one GODHEAD. See TRINITY.

tropology   A method of Bible study concerned with humankind's moral response to what is learned.

TULIP   An acronym for the five points of CALVINISM as delineated by John Calvin's followers at the Synod of Dort (1618–1619). The five points are: TOTAL DEPRAVITY, UNCONDITIONAL ELECTION, LIMITED ATONEMENT, IRRESISTIBLE GRACE, and the PERSEVERANCE OF THE SAINTS. See also CALVINISM, FIVE POINTS OF.

Twelve, Book of the   An ancient name for the twelve books of the MINOR PROPHETS, Hosea–Malachi, which were sometimes written on a single SCROLL.

Twelve, The   Shorthand for the twelve apostles, who were chosen by Jesus to be his disciples (Matt. 26:14; Luke 9:1, 12; John 6:67; Acts 6:2; 1 Cor. 15:5). The term appears frequently in Mark (3:16; 4:10; 6:7; 9:35; 10:32; 11:11; 14:10, 17, 20, 43).

two-source hypothesis   A proposed solution to the SYNOPTIC PROBLEM, which says that just two sources—Mark and Q—were used by Matthew and Luke. See also Q.

type   In biblical interpretation, a person, thing, or event that foreshadows or serves as a symbol of another person, thing, or event (called the ANTITYPE). For example, Melchizedek is

described as a type of Christ (Heb. 6:19–7:28). See also TYPO-
LOGICAL INTERPRETATION.

types of Christ   See TYPE.

typological interpretation   An approach to biblical interpretation that sees Old Testament persons, things, and events foreshadowing New Testament REVELATION by means of "types" (see
Rom. 5:14; 1 Cor. 10:2; Heb. 6:19–7:28). See also ANTITYPE and
TYPE.

U

Ugarit An ancient city on the northeastern coast of the Mediterranean, which flourished from approximately 1600 to 1200 B.C.E. as a commercial center and leader in maritime trade. The modern site is named Ras Shamra. Several Ugaritic stories illuminate biblical passages from the ancestral and settlement periods in the second millennium B.C.E.

Ugaritic An ancient SEMITIC language similar to HEBREW. See also SEMITIC LANGUAGES.

ultradispensationalism An extreme type of DISPENSA-TIONALISM, which believes the church began in Acts 13 or Acts 28. Also called hyperdispensationalism.

uncial Designating a style of Greek handwriting with large rounded letters, each separated from the next, like English capital letters, found especially in Old and New Testament manuscripts from the second to the eighth century. The term also applies to the letters themselves or a MANUSCRIPT written in this style.

unclean See CEREMONIALLY UNCLEAN.

unconditional election One of the five points of CALVIN-ISM (the "U" in TULIP), which asserts that God elected some for SALVATION solely on the basis of his grace and love, not on human merit or works. Also called unconditional predestination. See also CALVINISM, FIVE POINTS OF.

unconditional predestination   See UNCONDITIONAL ELECTION.

undisputed Pauline epistles   The books of Romans, 1 and 2 Corinthians, Galatians, Philippians, 1 Thessalonians, and Philemon, so named because their AUTHENTICITY as having been written by the APOSTLE Paul has rarely been questioned.

unforgivable sin   Shorthand for the "BLASPHEMY against the Holy Spirit," about which Jesus warned his listeners that it would not be forgiven (Matt. 12:31–32; Mark 3:28–29; Luke 12:10). In context, this warning may refer specifically to the accusation that Jesus operated under the power of BEELZEBUL. Some interpreters have understood Jesus' warning as applicable to persistent rejection of the truth of the GOSPEL, which is conveyed by the Holy Spirit.

united kingdom   Name used of ISRAEL during the reigns of Saul, David, and Solomon, before the kingdom was divided into northern and southern territories, each with its own ruler. See also DIVIDED KINGDOM.

universal church   The entirety of the body of Christ—all believers from all places and times. See also INVISIBLE CHURCH.

universal flood theory   The view that the GENESIS FLOOD (Gen. 6–8) encompassed the entire world and not merely a localized region. See also LOCAL FLOOD THEORY.

universalism   The view that all people will ultimately be saved and escape condemnation. See also PARTICULARISM.

unleavened bread   Bread that has been baked without LEAVEN (a fermentation-producing agent such as yeast), used in meals during the FEAST OF PASSOVER to remind the Israelites of the haste with which their ancestors fled Egypt (Ex. 12:8–20; Lev. 23:6–8). In RABBINIC LITERATURE leaven became a symbol of evil, a concept reflected also in New Testament texts (Matt. 16:6; Mark 8:15; Luke 12:1; 1 Cor. 5:6–8; Gal. 5:9). See also FEAST OF UNLEAVENED BREAD.

Unleavened Bread, Feast of   See FEAST OF UNLEAVENED BREAD.

unpardonable sin   See UNFORGIVABLE SIN.

unregenerate   Not BORN AGAIN by the Holy Spirit. See REGENERATION.

Urevangelium   A hypothetical ARAMAIC document that some scholars have thought was a common source of the SYNOPTIC GOSPELS (Germ., "primitive gospel").

Urim   See URIM AND THUMMIM.

Urim and Thummim   Gems or stones kept in the high priest's BREASTPIECE and used to discern God's will (Ex. 28:30; Num. 27:21; 1 Sam. 28:6). It is not entirely clear what the Urim and Thummim were or exactly how they were used.

Urmarkus   A hypothetical written source that some scholars think stands behind the Gospel of Mark (Germ., "primitive Mark"). Also Urmarcus.

U

V

variant   In TEXTUAL CRITICISM, a variation in the biblical text present in one or more manuscripts. There are hundreds of thousands of variants in the extant biblical manuscripts, but the vast majority of them are explainable and do not pose a problem in reconstructing the ORIGINAL wording of the Bible.

variant reading   See VARIANT.

Vaticanus   See CODEX VATICANUS.

vellum   High-quality writing material made from the skins of young animals. See also PARCHMENT.

verb   A word that describes an action or a state of being.

verbal aspect   See ASPECT.

verbal inspiration   View that divine INSPIRATION of the Scriptures extends to the very words of the biblical text, not merely to its ideas or principles.

version   In TEXTUAL CRITICISM, an early TRANSLATION of the Bible or a portion of the Bible. In New Testament textual criticism, for example, early versions include those in ARABIC, Coptic, Ethiopic, Latin, and Syriac, among others.

vicarious atonement The view of the ATONEMENT that Jesus died in place of sinners (Lat., *vicar,* "substitute").

vice list A catalog of sinful behavior presented for exhortation (e.g., Rom. 13:13; Gal. 5:19–21; Col. 3:5, 8; 1 Tim. 1:9–10; 2 Tim. 3:2–4; 1 Peter 2:1; 4:3).

virgin birth Mary's conceiving and bearing Jesus apart from sexual intercourse (Matt. 1:18–25; Luke 1:26–38). That Jesus was born of the "Virgin Mary" is mentioned in the APOSTLES' CREED.

virtue list A listing of positive, desirable qualities usually pertaining to moral excellence (e.g., Rom. 12:9–21; Gal. 5:22–23; 1 Tim. 2:8–10; Titus 1:6–9); the counterpart to a VICE LIST.

vision A divine disclosure, usually of spiritual realities, that resembles a trance or a dream (Gen. 15:1; Dan. 8–12; Hab. 2:2–3; Luke 1:22; Acts 10:1–17; 18:9; Rev. 9:17). Prophets, more so than the average person, were apt to experience visions (Num. 12:6; 1 Sam. 3:15; 2 Sam. 7:17).

vocative In Greek, the CASE used primarily for addressing someone. For example, the word "Father" in the LORD'S PRAYER is in the vocative case.

voice The feature of a VERB whereby its relationship to the SUBJECT is indicated, whether the action is directed toward the DIRECT OBJECT (ACTIVE VOICE) or toward the subject (PASSIVE VOICE). In Greek the MIDDLE VOICE frequently denotes REFLEXIVE verbal action directed by the subject and toward the subject.

V

Vorlage Any source document from which a TRANSLATION is made.

votive offering A somewhat broad descriptive term for a kind of sacrifice that involved a vow (Deut. 12:11, 17).

256

vowel pointing   The vowel system of Hebrew, written as small diacritical marks (dots, dashes, etc.) underneath, and sometimes inside or above, the consonant letters. Originally, written Hebrew had no vowels; in the second half of the first millennium the MASORETES, in an effort to preserve the sacred text, developed an elaborate system of vowel pointing, which is still preserved in modern editions of the Hebrew Bible.

Vulgate   The Latin VERSION of the Bible produced by Jerome (c. 347–420) at the end of the fourth century C.E.

V

wadi   A river valley, especially one that remains dry except during rainy season; or a stream that runs through such a channel.

Wager, the   An argument for the existence of God, attributed to Blaise Pascal (1623–1662), which states that one risks (i.e., wagers) less by believing in God than by not believing in him.

warfare, Christian   See SPIRITUAL WARFARE.

Washingtonensis   See CODEX WASHINGTONENSIS.

water baptism   See BAPTISM.

wave offering   The portion of the PEACE OFFERING that was given to the priest, which he then waved before the Lord as an act of worship (Ex. 29:24–27; Lev. 7:30, 34).

waw conjunctive   In Hebrew, a *waw* (the ninth letter of the alphabet) prefixed to nouns that links them together and is frequently translated "and." (The "w's" in *waw* are pronounced like the English "v's.") Also called the light *waw*, the simple *waw*, and the copulative *waw*.

waw consecutive   In Hebrew, a *waw* (the ninth letter of the alphabet), prefixed to certain verbs, which frequently denotes a series of consecutive events, epexegetical ideas, or various types of consequences (depending on context and on what sort of verbal form has the *waw*). (The "w's" in *waw* are pronounced like English "v's.") Also called a strong *waw* or a *waw* conversive.

***waw* disjunctive**   In Hebrew, a *waw* (the ninth letter of the alphabet) prefixed at the head of a clause to set it off from the surrounding text; frequently translated "but." (The "w's" in *waw* are pronounced like the English "v's.")

Way, the   In the book of Acts, a designation for the Christian community (9:2; 19:9, 23; 24:14, 22).

Weeks, Feast of   See FEAST OF WEEKS.

Western text-type   One of several text-types (a grouping of New Testament manuscripts with similar textual characteristics) thought to derive from the West, specifically Italy, Gaul, and North Africa, as well as Egypt and regions farther east. As the New Testament was copied and recopied, three distinct forms of the text, named for their supposed place of origin, developed: Byzantine, Western, and Alexandrian. See also ALEXANDRIAN TEXT-TYPE and BYZANTINE TEXT-TYPE.

whole offering   See BURNT OFFERING.

wisdom literature   A type of literature common in the ancient Middle East characterized by philosophical reflection, proverbial sayings, and analysis of life's experiences, human nature, religious devotion, and so on. In the Old Testament, the books of Job, Proverbs, and Ecclesiastes are wisdom literature (sometimes Psalms and Song of Songs are included). In the APOCRYPHA, the books of Sirach and Wisdom of Solomon are wisdom literature.

W

wisdom book   See WISDOM LITERATURE.

wise men   See MAGI.

witness   In TEXTUAL CRITICISM, a MANUSCRIPT, TRANSLATION, or quotation that is cited as evidence in a particular text-critical issue.

woe   An expression of reproach and lamentation for sinners that usually has several parts: the introductory formula "Woe to you" (or "Woe to those"), a recounting of the evil behavior that is the cause of the woe, and a warning about judgment. Woes occur frequently in prophetic literature (e.g., Isa. 5:8, 11, 18, 20–22; Jer. 22:13; Hab. 2:6, 9, 12, 15, 19), and in the Gospels on the lips of Jesus (e.g., Matt. 23:13–36).

Writings   The third division of the Hebrew Bible, after the LAW and the PROPHETS, including the books of Ruth, 1 and 2 Chronicles, Ezra, Nehemiah, Esther, Job, Psalms, Proverbs, Ecclesiastes, Song of Songs, Lamentations, and Daniel. Also called the KETUBIM.

works-righteousness   Pejorative shorthand term for human works (sometimes, "works of the Law") that are erroneously thought to earn divine favor, contributing in whole or in part to one's eternal salvation. The apostle Paul frequently discusses the impossibility of anyone pleasing God through works righteousness (Rom. 3:27–28; 4:1–25; Gal. 2:16; Eph. 2:9).

W

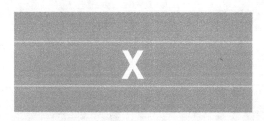

Xenophon   Greek historian who wrote early in the fourth century B.C.E.

Xerxes   King of Persia in the Achaemenid dynasty (486–465 B.C.E.). His name is rendered in some English versions "Ahasuerus" (Ezra 4:6; Est. 1:1; Dan. 9:1).

Yahweh   The name of God that occurs most frequently in the Hebrew Bible (over 6,800 times). This name, which was revealed to Moses at the burning bush (Ex. 3:13–15), likely derives from the root "to be," with the meaning "he is" or "he will be" (or from God's perspective, "I am"). Or it could be causative, underscoring God's creative activity. Because of its widespread usage, it is difficult to pin down exactly what "Yahweh" connotes, but scholars have suggested that it is God's COVENANT name, his personal name, or the cultic name (i.e., the name associated with TEMPLE worship and ritual). Most modern English translations render the Hebrew "LORD." See also DOCUMENTARY HYPOTHESIS, J, and YHWH.

Yahweh Elohim   Hebrew, "LORD God."

Yahwist   See J.

Yam Suph   Hebrew for SEA OF REEDS.

YHWH   Representation of the four Hebrew letters that spell the name of God that occurs most frequently in the Hebrew Bible (see YAHWEH). Medieval scribes, following a longstanding tradition, revered this particular name of God, substituting "ADONAI" ("Lord") instead when reading the biblical text aloud. Likewise a custom developed of placing the vowels for "Adonai" under these four consonants as a reminder to readers. Christians later transliterated this hybrid name as "JEHOVAH." The spelling "Yahweh," derived from YHWH, is undoubtedly closer to the original, although the precise pronunciation remains uncertain since the original Hebrew text contained no vowels. Called the sacred tetragram or tetragrammaton.

yod(h) The tenth letter of the Hebrew alphabet. It is the smallest letter of the alphabet, resembling an apostrophe. See also JOT.

yoke A device that encircles the necks of animals and harnesses their power for agricultural labor, especially plowing. In biblical times, the yoke became a symbol of oppression and slavery (Ex. 6:6–7; Hos. 10:11; 11:4; Gal. 5:1; 1 Tim. 6:1), or likewise of the negative results of SIN (Isa. 10:27; Lam. 1:14; Ezek. 34:27). Elsewhere it has a more positive sense, connoting ideas such as authority and correction (Lam. 3:27; Matt. 11:28–30).

Yom Kippur Hebrew for DAY OF ATONEMENT. Holy day falling on the tenth day of the first month, Tishri (corresponding to September/October), observed with prayer, CONFESSION, FASTING, and REPENTANCE. On Yom Kippur the HIGH PRIEST would offer an atoning SACRIFICE in the HOLY OF HOLIES for the forgiveness of Israel's sins (Lev. 16).

Y

Z

zealot In first-century PALESTINE, a member of a nationalistic Jewish party that believed in armed resistance against Rome and was hopeful of a revolution. A number of such resistance movements existed at various times during the New Testament era. It is unclear whether "Simon the Zealot" (Matt. 10:4; Mark 3:18; Luke 6:15; Acts 1:13) was actually a member of such a group or if he merely had fervent "zeal" for God.

ziggurat A large brick structure created by Mesopotamian peoples as a religious site or TEMPLE. Many think the Tower of Babel (Gen. 11) was a ziggurat.

Zion A designation used variously in the Hebrew Bible for the eastern hill of Jerusalem, which became the TEMPLE Mount (2 Sam. 5:7; Pss. 2:6; 76:2; Isa. 24:23), the entire city of Jerusalem (Isa. 40:9; 60:14; Joel 2:32), and metaphorically for the people of Israel (Isa. 3:16; Jer. 4:31). In the New Testament, the term refers once to the church (Heb. 12:22), but outside of Old Testament quotations it is rare. The etymology of the word is uncertain; various possibilities include "rock," "stronghold," "fortress," "dry place," and "running water."

Zoroastrianism A religious system associated with the Persian prophet Zoroaster (also spelled Zarathustra) that viewed the universe dualistically, with the forces of good and evil linked in combat in the parallel worlds of matter and SPIRIT. In the sixth

Z

century B.C.E. a form of Zoroastrianism became the official religion of the Persian Empire. Some scholars have suggested that certain biblical concepts—angels, the DEVIL, the eschatological clash of good and evil—seem to derive from Zoroastrian influence on JUDAISM.

zugoth The name given to pairs (Heb., "pairs") of rabbis who were thought traditionally to have transmitted the TORAH from the time of the MACCABEAN REVOLT to the first century C.E. Succeeded by the TANNAIM. Also zugot.

Zwinglianism Belief and practice derived from the teachings of the Swiss Protestant Reformer Ulrich Zwingli (1484–1531 C.E.).

We want to hear from you. Please send your comments about this book to us in care of zreview@zondervan.com. Thank you.

ZONDERVAN

ZONDERVAN.com/
AUTHORTRACKER
follow your favorite authors

9 780310 240341